Thom Browne

FASHION AUTEURS

Series Editors
Adam Geczy and Vicki Karaminas

Fashion Auteurs is a groundbreaking book series devoted to designers who have left an indelible mark on fashion history. Critical, clear and concise, each title, comprising around 30K words, is written by authorities in the field, situating each designer within their time and against their peers, with a focus on the contributions that have made them memorable. Using the term 'auteur' to designate film directors with a distinctive and influential style, this is the first series to treat fashion designers and related fashion creators (e.g. photographers) as on par with artists who have decisively shaped imagery, taste, and what is seen to be current and desirable. These books will be of interest not only to fashionistas and ardent devotees of fashion magazines but also to students and teachers of art and design, artists and designers themselves, not to mention anyone seeking a deeper acquaintance with fashion and design culture.

Forthcoming Titles in the Series
Judith Beyer, *Alessandro Michele*
Yuniya Kawamura, *Sebastian Masuda*

Thom Browne, 2024. UKinUSA, Wikimedia Commons.

Thom Browne

Benjamin Wild

ANTHEM PRESS

Anthem Press
An imprint of Wimbledon Publishing Company
www.anthempress.com

This edition first published in UK and USA 2026
by ANTHEM PRESS
75–76 Blackfriars Road, London SE1 8HA, UK
or PO Box 9779, London SW19 7ZG, UK
and
244 Madison Ave #116, New York, NY 10016, USA

British Library Cataloguing-in-Publication Data
A catalogue record for this book is available from the British Library.

Library of Congress Cataloging-in-Publication Data: 2025941607
A catalog record for this book has been requested.

ISBN-13: 978-1-83999-507-1 (Hbk) / 978-1-83999-508-8 (Pbk)
ISBN-10: 1-83999-507-6 (Hbk) / 1-83999-508-4 (Pbk)

This title is also available as an eBook.

CONTENTS

INTRODUCTION

Thom Browne. Without further prompting the name of this American designer is likely to conjure a distinctive clothed appearance. The ensemble that emerges in your mind might look something like the following ...

a grey twill three-buttoned jacket with a notch lapel and shortened sleeves that terminate approximately four inches above the wearer's wrist. A pair of corresponding slim-cut trousers hemmed at least one inch above the wearer's ankle. A crisp white Oxford shirt. A white pocket square tucked into the jacket's breast pocket, worn with a presidential fold. Subtlety polished crepe sole pebble grain black leather brogues. And, somewhere, perhaps dissecting the upper part of the left jacket sleeve or the left trouser leg, are four equally portioned white stripes. The banded rows are a conspicuous adornment although they maintain the almost monochromatic palette. More stipes, colourful ones – white, red, white, navy, white – which form the brand's grosgrain signature label, will probably feature on the wearer's socks, tie or tie bar.

Briefly sketched, the wardrobe you wear in your mind is an iconoclastic interpretation of the suit (Figure 0.1). It is simultaneously bland and blatant, familiar and unexpected. In a little over twenty years, this look has gained global followers – known as Browneans – and provoked detractors, who criticise one man's pedantry for imposing a uniform that dares to propose a new gender-neutral vision for the suit, a garment, seemingly inert and immutable, that has been the staple of men's wardrobes since the seventeenth century.[1] It is a look that has won Browne numerous awards, including 'Menswear Designer of the Year', which has been bestowed by the Council of Fashion Designers of America (CFDA) three times – in 2006, 2013, and 2016 – spawned collaborations with FC Barcelona, Brooks Brothers and Samsung, and seen him named as one of the world's most influential people by *Time* magazine in 2013. This influence was acknowledged in 2023, when he began his tenure as CFDA Chairman. In the same year, his *alma mater*, The University of Notre Dame, taught a one-credit module about his career, 'Strong Suits: The Art, Philosophy, and Business of Thom Browne'.[2] For his audacity, creativity and authority, Thom Browne is a deserving fashion *auteur*.

One of the most remarkable facts about Thom Browne's position within the fashion industry, and place within fashion history, is how quickly it has been attained. Fashion commentators talk confidently about Browne's 'world', 'universe' and 'empire' as though his ascendancy was assured, smooth. This was not the case. After graduating from the

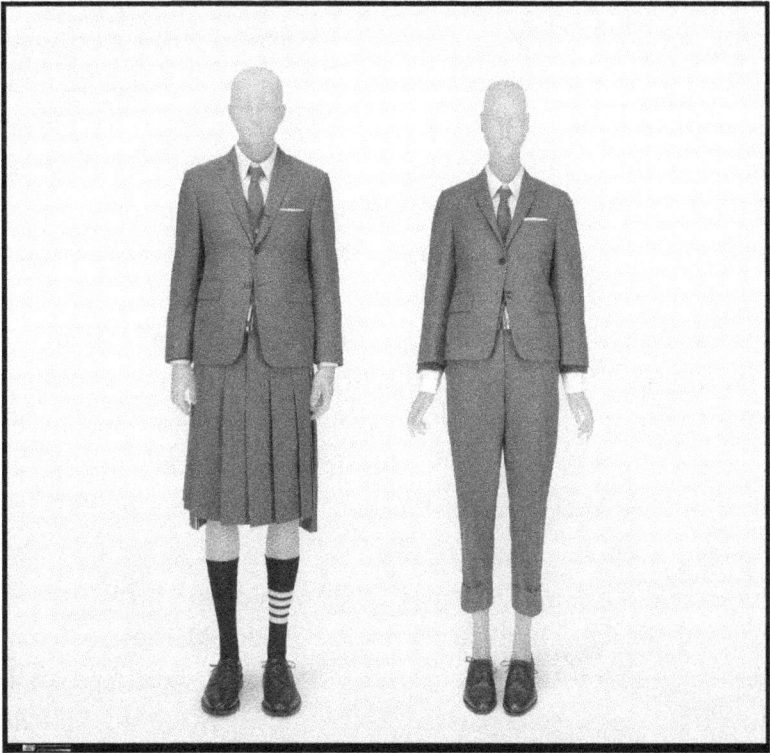

Figure 0.1 Thom Browne suit ensembles, 2018. Copyright of The Metropolitan Museum of Art/Art Resource/Scala, Florence.

University of Notre Dame and baulking at staid clerical jobs, Browne moved to Los Angeles where he dabbled at acting and styled vintage clothing with his friend, designer Johnson Hartig. Still restless, in 1997, he used the money raised from selling his car to move to New York. Now seemingly focussed on a career in fashion, Browne worked for Giorgio Armani and Ralph Lauren's Club Monaco, where he joined the branding and merchandising department. Four years later, in 2001, he created his own label with a collection of five suits. He sold these on an appointment-only basis from Manhattan's Meat-Packing district. To drum up interest in his wares, and because of the precarious nature of his fledging venture, Browne wore the suits around Manhattan as a form of marketing. He launched his first ready-to-wear men's collection in 2003 and staged his first runway show in 2005 as part of New York Fashion Week. Two years later, in 2007, he created a limited collection for women. A permanent ready-to-wear womenswear line was established in 2011. In 2013, he dressed the First Lady of the United States Michelle Obama for the second-term inauguration of President Barack Obama. In 2021, Browne expanded his clothing range to include children. In 2023, before an audience of 2002 cardboard cutouts identically clad in grey suits and blacked out sunglasses, he debuted his inaugural *haute couture* collection at *La Palais Garnier*, Paris (see Chapter 7). At the time of writing, in 2025, *Thom Browne* produces at least eight new collections a year and maintains 107 stores in forty countries around the world.[3]

All of this has been achieved within a twenty-two-year period, which included some of the gravest economic and political upheavals of living memory: the largest disruption to people's wealth since before the Second World War, the death of over seven million people due to COVID-19, and the rise of popularism within mainstream politics that continues to cause global fragmentation and fuel sectarian violence, both physical and psychological. The rapidity of the brand's expansion, the simple fact of its survival, makes Browne's accomplishment surer, but it should not create a false impression of ease. In 2009, Browne came perilously close to bankruptcy. Accolades won and collaborations forged belie the reality that financial security for the company was only attained in 2018, when Italian luxury fashion house Ermenegildo Zegna acquired an 85 per cent stake in the business, which was then valued at $500 million.

The commercial viability and conceptual influence of Thom Browne is even more remarkable because the designer has no formal training in designing or clothes-making. He admits that he can't illustrate, 'at all'. New collections begin with Browne using plastic shape templates to give rudimentary form to his thinking. He explains that 'a pleated skirt would be a triangle. A square would be more of a shorter jacket. A rectangle would be more of an outerwear piece'.[4] Subsequent meetings with his team produce more recognisable, and workable, design sketches. Mood boards are never used, however, because Browne insists it is better – freer – to work by closing the eyes and imagining.[5]

At the very beginning, Browne developed his quintet of suits through a year-long process of experimentation with Italian tailor Rocco Ciccarelli. Ciccarelli had emigrated to the United States during the 1950s and established his own brand, Rocco Ciccarelli Custom Tailoring. Schooled in the traditions of men's tailoring, Ciccarelli initially considered Browne 'crazy'. The Italian admired the American's commitment to a sartorial vision, but he did not hesitate to depart from Browne's puritanical measurements. On the sly, he kept the length of suit sleeves longer to ensure wearers would 'feel free in the suit'. Browne and Ciccarelli formed a close working relationship until the latter's retirement in 2015, by which point the Thom Browne uniform had been confidently established.[6]

The look is all of Browne's own. In interviews, the designer is assertive in claiming 'it's all about me'.[7] The playfulness and pedantry evidenced by his uniform's shortened hemlines reveals the influence of America's preppie style, which he experienced, and experimented with, during his university years. Browne followed his father and sister to Notre Dame, a private Catholic university in Indiana, where he studied accountancy. Thoughts of pursuing a business career like that fictionalised in Sloan Wilson's largely autobiographical best-selling novel of 1955, *The Man In The Grey Flannel Suit*, may have been on Browne's mind. The influence of sport was probably greater. At Notre Dame, he continued to swim competitively. He had started when he was six. For four years, he maintained a three-day training regime that involved twelve hours of weekly swimming. Now, he runs. Daily spurts typically cover eight miles and last for a little over an hour. For Browne, running has become an exercise rather than a sport because it is not competitive.[8] The distinction seems important to understand Browne's mentality and motivation as a designer. His keen interest in physical exertion, and the effort required to sustain this, are reflected in his determination as a business owner and his concern for what he believes to be correct proportion.

The clarity with which Browne articulates his ideas – his vision – through clothing designs, runway shows and interviews is occasionally unnerving. His commitment to proportion, which is inspired by 'an almost classic idea' and 'a superhuman body', might even seem repugnant as the fashion industry, and global society, shows greater commitment to challenge the constructs of gender and move away from socialised binaries that have informed 'western' thinking since at least the nineteenth century.[9] Browne is aware that his ideas about proportion are not shared by everyone. He experienced people's laughter when he wore his suits in Manhattan in 2001. He claims people still laugh now. He acknowledges his competitiveness – stubbornness – and that his route through the fashion industry has been his own. Nonetheless, he still admits confusion about why people don't see his clothes and think, 'Oh, wow – I can relate to this.'[10] The comment is revealing because it evidences the deeply personal connection between Browne and his eponymous brand. It demonstrates that the company Browne has established advocates his personal outlook – philosophy might be too formal a term – as equally as it does his preferred aesthetic.

The iconoclastic nature of Browne's contribution to fashion and his personal resoluteness means that there are no ready parallels to make among his predecessors or peers (Figure 0.2). His life partner, the Wendy Yu curator in charge of the Costume Institute of the Metropolitan Museum of Art, New York, Andrew Bolton has likened him to fashion designer Gabrielle Chanel for the clarity and thoroughness through which he has defined and maintains a sartorial code.[11] Subsequent chapters argue that it is simpler, and probably more accurate, to identify Browne's influences, which are diverse, rather than seek to place him along some kind of fashion or tailoring trajectory, where he is presented as an heir to Giorgio Armani, say, who deconstructed the suit in the 1970s.[12]

Bolton is surely right to emphasise ideas and the intangible in explaining the uniqueness and importance of Browne's place within the contemporary fashion industry and fashion history. Whilst he is famous, or notorious, for his designs, and the truncated suit in particular, this book will make the case that Browne does not fit comfortably within a design tradition or canon. The designer and his eponymous brand are best understood on their terms. There is a danger that this argument revitalises the 'western' myth of 'great men', or in the case of fashion designers, the *sui generis*, of which there is an equally long tradition.[13] This approach may also imply partiality towards

Figure 0.2 Thom Browne suit ensemble, 2007. Copyright of Victoria and Albert Museum, London.

Browne, with the attendant risk that he might slide from the analytical hook.

To emphasise difference is fundamental to show how the creative and commercial value of Thom Browne's world depends on the increasingly inseparable link between the brand and the man himself.[14] The brand has become like a prism that refracts all the designer wants would-be Browneans to know about him, his sartorial vision and values.

The method adopted in this book, which pays attention to public interviews, show notes, the design and presentation of Browne's collections, is consequently useful in highlighting inconsistencies within the designer's character and the work he produces. It also helps to explain what might appear to be one of the biggest paradoxes within the world Browne has created. Namely, how can the extreme rigour and discipline of his tailoring be reconciled to the whimsical and fantastical accessories that his brand produces – notably the Hector bag, which is based on his wire-haired dachshund (Figure 7.1) – the storytelling and spectacular choreography of runway shows through which his designs are first shared.

The deeply personal nature of Browne's work, and his desire that audiences see things on his terms, certainly pose a challenge for people who want to engage with the brand. Various journalists have expressed feeling 'alienated' by his runway shows. Tim Blanks, *Business of Fashion* editor-at-large, suggests Browne's shows are 'defiant' and sometimes make audience members want to 'shriek [their] head off'.[15]

Occasionally, audience members have walked out of shows.[16] Browne is unapologetic. He maintains that the rigour of the shows, their detail and length, are an important part of what he wants to share about his practice and outlook. Meeting Browne on his terms is evidently a litmus test for would-be Browneans.

As alienating as they might appear, the challenge, provocation and visual spectacle of Browne's runways are an important element in establishing his work as an art form where, in Blanks's phrase, Browne exists as 'impresario'. The designer claims to love the tension that he can evoke through his shows. Discomforting audiences seems to be an integral part of his aim to pull them out of their world and make them see something different through his storytelling. This stridency and demonstration of will mean that his runway productions provide a personal insight into Browne's thinking. Whilst superficially fanciful and other-worldly, the shows are largely consistent for being a paean to the values of the twentieth-century America in which he grew up. Industrious, sober-minded (and suited) people with an uncomplicated, strong morality delight in community and cohesion. The premise of these shows seems oblivious to the fact that the pursuit of a more creative and hopeful place is predicated on a privilege and inequality that will exclude more people than it can actually embrace. In this sense, the world Browne has created, precisely because it is so personal, is not as benign as he might believe. If a customer wants to wear Browne's stripes, they need to earn them.

The ascendancy of *Thom Browne* has been charted in numerous articles, interviews and films. To celebrate the first twenty years of the brand Andrew Bolton published a 'comprehensive monograph'. This 420-page tome is more photo album, a compendium of fashion memories, than critique. It contains only one essay, authored by Bolton, which focuses on a live presentation-cum-*tableau* that Browne staged as part of *Pitti Uomo Immagine* in June 2009 to explain the designer's manifesto. In this sense, the book constitutes something of an official record of how Browne wishes to see – and wishes readers to interpret – his eponymous brand's formative years. The apparent orthodoxy of the volume is underscored by its author. Bolton is Browne's life partner and, like him, wears only *Thom Browne* clothing, in public and private.[17] Whilst Bolton writes as scholar and curator, his position is not dispassionate. His involvement in this anniversary project indicates that he has an integral position within the creation and maintenance of the Brownean world.[18]

Consequently, this book, which considers Browne as an *auteur*, is the first to analyse his designs and evaluate his wider contribution to fashion and the fashion industry. Four collections, spanning the past twenty years, form the focus of the chapters that follow. I start with two chapters that set the sartorial scene. They consider, first, Thom Browne's world. This involves a comparison of the *Pitti Uomo Immagine* performance, which is analysed in Bolton's monograph, and a presentation that was produced for the *Salone del Mobile* during Milan Design Week in April 2024. Joint discussion of these set pieces enable us to understand the world of Thom Browne that we are about to enter, and how it has changed during the course of this Millennium. Chapter 2 narrows the chronological and spatial focus to consider the importance of American influence within Browne's designs. Chapters 3–6 discuss four collections that elucidate different elements of Browne's oeuvre: Spring ready-to-wear 2014, which appeared to take inspiration from sixteenth-century English fashions; Fall ready-to-wear 2020, which was inspired by the Old Testament Bible story of Noah's Ark; Fall ready-to-wear 2023, which re-interpreted Antoine de Saint-Exupéry's novella, *Le Petit Prince* (*The Little Prince*), first published in 1943, and Thom Browne's first *haute couture* collection for Fall 2023. Chapter 7 brings the threads, and paradoxes, of Browne's sartorial story together by considering the conspicuous place of accessories within his catwalk and commercial collections.

Chapter 1

THOM BROWNE'S WORLD

Many fashion commentators insist that Thom Browne's greatest achievement as a designer is the creation of a 'world' or 'universe' that embodies his vision of fashion and the lifestyle that maintains it. Depending on how far these authorities think his strictures on proportion are benign or malevolent, he is either a munificent ruler, who enables people to experience clothing – the suit particularly – in a way that becomes liberating, or a despot, who seeks to bind wearers to his version of sartorial perfection. Since 2005, Browne's collections, their accompanying runways, press interviews and commentaries have cumulatively shaped the dimensions and appearance of this world, and not always, one suspects, in ways that he has welcomed. Browne's runway shows have frequently caused confusion and consternation among fashion journalists, whose questioning narratives threaten the coherence of his domain.

On two occasions, in 2009 and 2024, Browne intervened to clarify his sartorial intentions. These interventions have taken the form of carefully choreographed visual set pieces. The first was a live *tableau* that formed part of *Pitti Uomo Immagine*. The second, which was intended as an homage to this event, was a presentation that coincided with his brand's collaboration with Italian linen company *Frette*.[19] Andrew Bolton has likened the *Pitti tableau* to a manifesto. He has analysed this event in a solo essay published within a book that celebrates the first two decades of *Thom Browne*. The more recent presentation, created in Browne's twentieth anniversary year, has many similarities to this live event. Consequently, it is viewed here as something akin to a manifesto refresh. Analysed together, the two events elucidate the development of Thom Browne's world over the past two decades. They are an ideal place to start an analysis of Browne as a fashion *auteur*.

Pitti Uomo Immagine, 14 June 2009

The *tableau* that Thom Browne staged at *Pitti Uomo Immagine*, his debut European show, was monotonous. Intentionally so. The presentation, which lasted for a little over fourteen minutes, used the *Aula Magna* in Florence's *Istituto di Scienze Miltari Aeronautiche* as backdrop.[20] In a large, sombre hall with lacquered parquet flooring four rows of ten desks were arranged before a single desk that was positioned slightly apart. The desks were of dark, subtly polished metal that contained rows of drawers on each side.

A small, four-legged grey chair with cushioned seating and back pads was positioned between the drawers. An *Olivetti* typewriter was centrally placed on each of the desks. To the left of the machine was a pile of blank white A4-paper. A single business card had been placed to its right. At the left side of each desk, when viewed from the perspective of its sitter, there was a floor-length chrome coat stand. A mid-grey *Thom Browne* cardigan with four white banded stripes on the left arm hung from each. In the case of the single desk, the coat stand was positioned to the sitter's right. The arrangement of the single desk differed in two further respects. First, it had a brass table bell instead of a business card. Second, a slim black and metal briefcase had been placed to the left side of the chair. The scene was redolent of Hollywood depictions of offices from mid-century America, the era of Mad Men. There is a particularly strong resemblance to scenes from the 1967 movie *Play Time*, directed by Jacques Tati. The film, which required the construction of a set known as 'Tativille', involves characters moving between scenes in a grey hued metropolis of glass, steel and concrete. On either side of Browne's more modest set, an audience of fashion journalists stood behind a discrete cordon.

What followed was a plotless drama of two acts, punctuated by eight bell rings. The presentation started when a white man approached the coat stand of the single, front desk. He wore a grey two-piece *Thom Browne* suit, a khaki overcoat and black leather Derbies. The man took off his coat and grey suit jacket and hung them upon the coat stand. He replaced these layers with the cardigan. After spending almost a minute buttoning and flattening the garment, he seated himself at the desk, and rang the bell. Forty white male models, who wore an identical outfit to the first man, entered the hall from his left. The sound was loud as the men's footsteps echoed around the interior. The models had different coloured-hair, but looked similar. Their hair was parted from the left and they all wore *Thom Browne* black half-rimmed horn spectacles. Filling each row at a time, from right to left, the men put down the briefcase they carried in their right hand, and stood to attention behind a desk, facing front. When the first man rang the bell a second time, the men removed their suit jacket and coat, replacing them with the cardigan. A third bell ring, and the men commenced typing. The sound, at once rhythmic and indistinct, was intense. After a little under one minute, four white men appeared from the left of the front desk. These men were without coats. They wore grey shorts and corresponding suit jackets. Black knee-high socks matched their shoes. From right to left, the men walked to end of a different row and began to collect a single sheet of paper that the model typists removed from their typewriters. When the collectors had reached the front of their respective row, and gathered all sheets, they transferred their paper pile to the front desk, and left the way they had come. After their exit, the man seated behind the front desk stood, walked to its front and collected the papers into a single stack. He returned to his seat and rang the bell a fourth time. At this prompt, the men stopped typing and reached for their briefcases.

They removed a red apple, which they placed near the upper right corner of their desk. They then removed a folded brown paper bag and, from within this, a smaller sealed cellophane bag that contained a sandwich. They ate, leaning into their briefcases, until the fifth bell chimed. The men resumed typing after they had returned the sandwich to the briefcase, and the briefcase to the floor. The sequence with the paper collectors was repeated. After almost eleven minutes since the first man appeared, he struck the bell twice. This was the cue for the typists to stop work and stand behind their desks. A seventh bell prompted them to re-dress themselves. The eighth and final bell instructed the men to file out of the hall, row by row, as they had entered. As each man passed the front desk, he left behind his red apple.

This lengthy description captures the monotony and discipline of Browne's presentation. It is a scene – a world – in which almost everything is grey, controlled and constrained, from the men's actions to their cropped garments. Bolton describes the presentation as a 'manifesto' that was 'unapologetic and uncompromising'.[21] The manifesto announced through this presentation was the Browne uniform (Figure 0.1). The grey two-piece suit, its proportions and styling, chiefly the monochromatic banded stripes and white-red-white-blue-white grosgrain ribbon stripes, and accompanying dress accessories, like the tie-bar and spectacles. In declaring his sartorial position, and demonstrating the rigour that it would take to maintain, Bolton suggests that Browne was the first designer to provide such a 'decisive, definitive, and determined' stance since Gabrielle Chanel. Like her, Browne's work 'railed against the exigencies of fashion'.[22]

Bolton argues that the key to Browne's protest is located in his use of grey. The colour derives power from the fact that it is typically overlooked on account of being undefinable and unremarkable.[23] But grey is mercurial. Less noisy than other, more popular colours, it allows its subjects to express themselves with greater clarity. Bolton suggests that it is an ideal colour for the socially digitised and public lives that many people now live. When worn on the body, grey enables 'its wearer to be a public person with a private life, someone with private thoughts and private feelings'.[24] This point is evident from the *Pitti Uomo Immagine* presentation. The monotony of this fourteen-minute non-event did heighten the model's individuality, albeit subtly. During a runway show, which can last for a similar length of time, models are rarely noticed, their uniqueness is not immediately apparent. In this *tableau*, because the models were identically dressed, their personalities were, briefly, noticeable. The man who sat at the front desk had a tattoo around his right wrist and wore an elaborate silver ring on the ring finger of his right hand. Whilst distinctions between the other male models were harder to spot, their identical clothing emphasised how they removed their coats differently, typed differently, ate their sandwiches differently – a few seemed genuinely hungry – and, at the end, as they walked off the set and had to place their red apple in an ever-diminishing space on the front desk, it was possible to see them calculate the spatial distances that remained. One model chose poorly. His apple rolled to the floor, despite the subtle efforts of another model who tried to retrieve it without breaking rank and bringing chaos into the calm.[25]

The apple, which is conventionally used to represent the fruit that Adam and Eve ate to gain knowledge and commit Original Sin, is an apt symbol to reflect the limit of Browne's omnipotence over his creation. Nonetheless, the event emphasised the importance of colour, proportion, discipline and their interdependence. The power of the grey cloth used by Browne is only discernible because of the proportions to which it is shaped and cut. In turn, the proportions reflect the discipline of the wearers' lives, more so in the case of them being models. Consequently, whilst grey might be appropriate for all people, the proportions and discipline that Browne's uniform requires begins to exclude. This unsettling point is addressed in Browne's installation of 2024, which constitutes something of a manifesto refresh.

Salone del Mobile, 'Time to Sleep', April 2024

Thom Browne's short, barely ten-minute presentation during Milan Design Week, made use of another Italian location, the Grand Hall of Honour of the *Palazzina Appiani*, a former family home of the French Emperor Napoleon Bonaparte, in Milan. In a wide, high-ceiled room, decorated with ornate friezes and two large glass chandeliers, six metal-framed beds were aligned before a wall punctuated with five floor-to-ceiling windows.[26] Between them, four tall mirrors were affixed to the wall. Two director's chairs had been placed in the corners of the room, in front of the first and fifth windows. The glass panes were open but the outside was concealed behind closed slatted shutters. The mattress on each bed had a light grey cover decorated with four white banded stripes that ran across its width. There was a white fitted sheet beneath the mattress and a white pillow on top, which had been placed at the head of the bed nearest to the windows. An eye mask, covered in the same grey fabric as the mattress, was positioned in the centre of the pillow. A chrome coat stand was placed on the floor between the end of each bed and wall. They were identically hung with a white shirt, a grey jacket and pair of shorts, a grey cardigan and tie. Frédéric Chopin's *'Nocturne in C-Sharp Minor'* played as the audience surveyed the space.

The plot within the presentation, which was as eventless as the *Pitti* performance, began when a white male model entered the room from the left. He was dressed entirely in *Thom Browne* clothing: a grey suit jacket, shorts, white shirt, tie, black socks and shoes. The model completed one and a half circuits of the beds and paused between the third and fourth, facing the audience. He looked at his watch-less left wrist as if to check the time, and then exited the room from the left door. Upon his exit, the room darkened. Shortly after, the man returned. He walked along the back of the room, against the windows and stopped in front of the far right director's chair. Unseen, another man had already occupied a standing position in front of the director's chair in the left corner of the room. Just over a minute and a half into the presentation, the room brightened and the music changed to Piotr Tchaikovsky's '*Valse de la Belle Au Bois Dorman*'. Six models filed into the space from the left door – a white female, a white male, a black female, a white male, an Asian female and a black male. The models were dressed in similar white undergarments that consisted of a vest top and shorts, black knee-length socks and leather shoes. They walked the perimeter of the room, closest to the audience, and stopped when they were each standing before one of the beds and coat stands. Simultaneously, they began to dress. Putting on the white shirt, shorts, tie, cardigan and jacket. When dressed, they turned to face the wall-mounted mirrors. At this point, the men occupying the director's chairs emerged from the shadowy corners to review the models' attire. They worked diligently from the outside to the centre, each inspecting three models. When their review was complete, the six models walked to the left side of their beds, which they sat upon. The two men, who had recently inspected the somnolent models, proceeded to place an eye-mask over their faces. Again, they commenced their work from the outer beds. As soon as their eye-mask was secured, the models reclined fully and crossed their arms over their torso. The two facilitators returned to their chairs. The music changed for a third time and Johannes Brahms' '*Wiegenlied*' started to play. After almost ninety seconds, a snoring sound was preceded by the ringing of an alarm bell. As Johann Sebastian Bach's '*Minuet in G Major*' started to play, the models, in turn, had their eye-masks removed (Figure 1.1). They got up from their beds and undressed, repeating their pre-sleep routine in reverse order. When they were again wearing their white vest and shorts, they filed out of the room, retracing the steps of their entry. As the lighting darkened and the music changed for a final time to play Johann Sebastian Bach's '*Cello Suite no. 3 in C Major*', the male facilitators came forward to flatten and straighten each of the beds. When their task was complete, they too exited the room.

Like the *Pitti* event, this presentation was monotonous. A sequence happens and is repeated. Where a single bell controlled models in the live event, a combination of bell, models and props informed the action of this presentation. The musical score and undulating lighting made the installation less austere, but the actions of the models were no less controlled. They were, however, much freer. Annotations that accompany the presentation on the *Thom Browne* website explain that the models 'dress for the work of their dreams'. The grey suit becomes a transportation device that makes possible their wearers' 'voyage to the dream world'.[27] In interviews, the designer said he had wanted to 'challenge the audience to question the role of dress in public life'.[28] In this framing, the *Thom Browne* suit explicitly becomes a device of liberation. It is the means by which people enter a world of their choosing. The presentation visually represents Bolton's argument that the grey suit confers individuality by

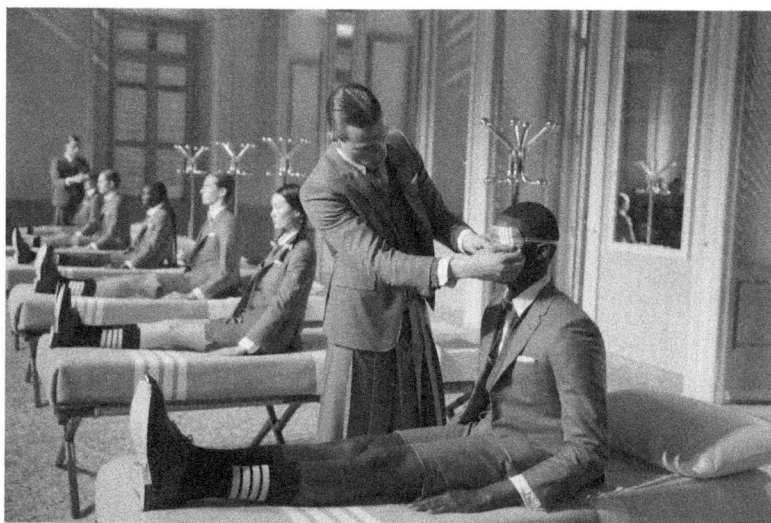

Figure 1.1 Thom Browne 'Time to Sleep' presentation with Frette at Palazzina Appiani, 2024. Photograph by Stefania M. D'Alessandro/ Getty Images for Thom Browne.

concealing, or suppressing, inessential noise. This is a much more upbeat interpretation of the suit than that offered in 2009. In this earlier performance, models were only free of the drudgery of typing before they had donned the suit jacket and after they had taken it off. The positivity of the *Salone del Mobile* presentation and its greater humanity is also reflected in the choice of models. Instead of a phalanx of white men, there are men and women of different races. In 2009, Browne had yet to create a women's line – although he had experimented with a women's collection in 2007. The lack of racial diversity in this earlier performance is no less explicable, although the 2024 casting does show that Browne's world has become marginally more inclusive during the intervening fifteen years.

The *Salone del Mobile* presentation conveys a more upbeat message because it refreshes the *Thom Browne* manifesto by clarifying the benefits that adherents (wearers) derive, rather than singly proclaiming the vision of the Godhead (Browne). However, where it gives, it also takes back, or rather grasps more firmly. The diversity of models, by sex and race, and the emphasis on benefits heightens the importance of proportion and discipline. A wider, if still limited, group of people are included within Browne's world. These models still possess the 'superhuman' bodies that fascinates the designer, and which require discipline to maintain. The vision that Browne presented during Milan Design Week may be more enticing than that offered fifteen years earlier, but it is no easier to achieve. The installation's expanded cast visibly demonstrates the enlargement of Browne's world, which now includes a womenswear line, but all would-be Browneans are expected to embody rigour and resolve. Consequently, Browne's world remains exclusive, elitist and all of his own.

The collaboration with *Frette* came about because Browne has the company's linens in his New York home. For him, the partnership was easy. 'I know exactly what I want and how it relates to the world I've created [...] Beautifully created products that I want my customers to experience the same way I do.'[29] Browne's insistence on speaking to his customers so they can understand his intentions was likened to 'fun', but in the designer's world, the fun is on his terms:

> Yes, in a way, unfortunately, I can't get away from it. It's all one world. I like people to feel the connection between what I do for my collections but also my personal life and all things that I really like myself, and that's what makes it easy and fun to do because it's so personal. And I think it's more valuable to people, too because it is personal.[30]

Chapter 2

THOM BROWNE'S AMERICA

If Thom Browne has created a sartorial world, it is America writ large. His personal approach to fashion design means the proportions, colours and details that make his uniform are rooted in the associations and memories of his upbringing and family, which he describes as 'classic, quintessential Middle America'.[31] Much of Browne's inspiration comes from the preppie aesthetic, a derivation of Ivy League style that emerged within the campuses and on the sports fields of America's Ivy League universities during the early twentieth century. The Ivy look is at once casual and considered. Soft, unstructured tailoring – emphasising athleticism and jouissance through the combination of contrasting textures, colours and patterns – is underpinned by stealthy attention to detail that includes the depth of a lapel, the length of turn-ups on trousers and an eagle-eyed awareness of certain brands, notably Brooks Brothers, J. Press and Bass.[32] Ivy style was intimately associated with privilege and America's north-eastern coast, where its wearers lived and leisured.

The preppie style, which emerged during the 1950s and 1960s, is arguably a more colourful and commercial interpretation of the Ivy look. It was popularised by John F. Kennedy, who became America's thirty-fifth president in 1960, and, reflecting its global influence, the Duke of Windsor, who reigned as Edward VIII of the United Kingdom for 326 days in 1936.[33] Having champions of this social status meant the preppie look retained the elitist and privileged aspirations of Ivy look even after its prominence had begun to wane. By the 1970s, the appeal of preppie style was also dwindling. The decline was temporary and probably a reflection of social unease within the United States, fuelled by political and racial division, economic stagnation and disenfranchisement with the ongoing Vietnam War. It was during this period that Ralph Lauren established his eponymous brand, starting with a collection of men's ties. Calvin Klein did likewise with his namesake brand, which was launched with a collection of coats. By the early 1980s, buoyed by an economic upturn, preppie found new adherents. In 1986, Lauren opened his brand's first flagship store in Manhattan. Two years prior, Tommy Hilfiger had launched his namesake brand with a bag in the colours of the American flag (red–white–blue).[34]

Browne credits Lauren and Klein as being among the most influential designers to create an 'American sensibility' in dress.[35] Born in 1965, he would have been in university when these brands were becoming established and re-imagining fashion, preppie included, for a new generation. Browne's years at Notre Dame appear to have been an important period for the germination of a personal aesthetic that would now be considered quintessentially Brownean. Apparently, he would shrink vintage clothing in a dryer to achieve the truncated proportions that he desired and which now characterise his suits.[36] His brand's grosgrain label, which is inspired by the ribbon attached to swimming medals, can be traced to his years competing with Notre Dame's swimming team. In 2022, when Browne produced a twelve-piece capsule collection with the menswear online retailer *Mr Porter*, he suggested that his interpretation of the varsity jacket, tie and sports blazer had a uniquely American sensibility, which is 'what I would have worn at Notre Dame'.[37] Through these two examples alone, there seems to be an emergence of the discipline and whimsy that define his collections. Reflecting on his clothing history, Browne has suggested that his designs convey 'a very Ivy League sensibility, taken to an almost-uptight level of aesthetic, which is funny to play with'.[38]

Browne's observation of his work was reflected in the placement of two of his ensembles from 2018 in the first element of a two-part exhibition *In America: A Lexicon of Fashion* organised by the Costume Institute of the Metropolitan Museum of Art, New York, in 2021. The exhibition was conceived to commemorate the seventy-fifth anniversary of the Institute's foundation and to establish 'a modern vocabulary of American fashion'.[39] Andrew Bolton argued that unlike European dress, which is often described as possessing an emotional resonance, American dress is fated to be merely practical. Whilst this may make it egalitarian, Bolton suggests the reductive assessment marginalises the artistry, ingenuity and sophistry of America's clothing designers.[40] It is also a judgement that does not satisfactorily explain the dynamic relationship between American clothing and the American nation. Consequently, the exhibition was conceived to embody the bricolage-like construction of a patchwork quilt, where contrast characterises the constituent parts and cohesion and unity define the finished textile. Within the exhibition, garments were grouped Linnaeus-like into twelve word-based sections that were variously subdivided under a further ninety-nine different words. Browne's grey-tailored suits—one dressed on a male mannequin with a jacket and skirt, and one dressed on a female mannequin with a jacket and trousers—appeared under the category of 'Discipline', within the 'Strength' section (Figure 0.1). The designs were described as 'rooted in the inventive adaptation of classic forms', where traditional materials and convention were 'shifted' to demonstrate that the 'regularity' of a sartorial uniform was not 'delimiting'.[41]

It is probably misleading to see *In America: A Lexicon of Fashion* as a replay of the Battle of Versailles Fashion Show, which took place on 28 November 1973. To raise funds for the renovation of the Palace of Versailles, five French fashion designers and five American designers organised a runway show within the former royal residence. Against expectations – or prejudices – the Americans were widely heralded as the winners.[42] Significant as the event was for demonstrating the skill of American designers, three of whom – Bill Blass, Stephen Burrows and Halston – had their works featured in *In America: A Lexicon of Fashion*, the Costume Institute's exhibition demonstrates that the artistry of American fashion designers has continued to fare poorly in comparison to their European counterparts. For Thom Browne, whose sartorial reference point is chiefly America, this situation is anathema. Since becoming Chair of the Council of Fashion Designers of America (CFDA) in 2023, he has been working to challenge narratives that imply American fashion prioritises commerce over creativity.[43] Like an *auteur* who exerts a strong influence over multiple aspects of their work, Browne is seeking to make the case that fashion exists in dialogue, and on equal standing, with other forms of art.

In December 2023, Browne approached auction house Sotheby's to curate an exhibition that would 'hammer home the idea of American fashion as art'.[44] For Sotheby's January 2024 iteration of their 'Visions of America' auction, Browne curated an exhibition of nine items that included Charles Willson Peale's portrait of George Washington and a Qing dynasty bowl, recognising that an American sensibility in art does not exist in a cultural vacuum.[45] For the first time, the annual Sotheby's auction included an online fashion sale, 'CFDA: Defining American Style', organised by the CFDA that featured work from thirty-seven of its members. The items included examples of American fashion from the 1970s to the present from Oscar de la Renta, Ralph Lauren, Tom Ford, Jason Wu, Christian

Siriano and Thom Browne, among others.[46] Proceeds from the sale funded CFDA education initiatives aimed at supporting future fashion designers.

Altruistic as this initiative was, its execution reflected Browne's personal tastes. When explaining his involvement, he spoke repeatedly of his choices being 'instinctive'. His selection of nine items for the exhibition reflected: 'what I would consider important for me, because I think the most important thing about the sale, since I am curating, is that people see my taste, and what I specifically choose, like, really represents what I would actually choose for myself'.[47]

This outlook, which chimes with how Browne spoke about his *Salone del Mobile* presentation, underscores the control, discipline and perhaps solipsism, with which his American-centred world is constructed.[48]

This begs a question: How accessible and appealing is Browne's America? In response to his Spring 2008 collection, which 'exploded the masculine certitudes of patrician Americana', in the words of journalist Tim Blanks, *The New York Times* journalist S. Bridges suggested that Browne had presented a vision of America's 'diminishment'.[49] For them, the designer's interpretation of 'classic American symbols' such as the blazer, jersey and Oxford shirt, was 'perverse'. Instead of reflecting 'the good life', which is how these aspirational objects of apparel are conventionally portrayed within the Ivy League and preppie canon, the objects challenged assumptions about their social signification. Bridges cites one ensemble where shirt sleeves were so long that they protruded through the armholes of a jacket to be knotted together behind the model's back, restricting the movement of their arms. Unlike Ralph Lauren, who has spread a sartorial vision of America that is colourful, nonchalant and privileged, Bridges suggests that Browne's approach is more interrogative.[50] To an extent, he is right. Browne has made it clear that he 'ha[s] no interest in being just another designer. I [want] people to respond, negatively or positively'.[51]

The personal nature of Browne's designs, along with an apparent ambivalence to how they are interpreted, makes it difficult, potentially misleading, to attribute a clear intention and strategy to him. Nonetheless, it might be possible to argue that Browne conceives of his designs, framed by the breezy, aspirational aesthetics of the preppie look, to question how American values in the present have shifted from those of his past. Viewing the world through the prism of his 'ultra American family' and upbringing, it may be that Browne is inadvertently conceiving his designs through anachronistic comparison.[52] The concept of anachronistic comparison was coined by philosopher and art historian Georges Didi-Huberman. He argued that anachronism is a useful analytical tool because it provides 'a shock, a tearing of the veil' that calls into question '*what-goes-without-saying*' in a society.[53] By way of elaboration, Didi-Huberman suggested that pieces of art should be studied as 'manipulators of time', for two reasons. First, time continually redefines experiences of objects, which are constructed through people's memories.[54] A memory can be a recollection that directly involves the object in question or it can be something entirely unrelated that is sparked by the object. Second, artists have always referenced times beyond their own when making objects, such that they become 'an artist of the *more-than-past* of memory'.[55]

Browne's designs always appear to have their origins in the past, because of his focus on traditional tailoring and proportion, and visual interest in the preppie style, but in both cases, he twists, even tears, connections between history and present through personal reinterpretation. Consequently, the America that emerges is, like his clothing, at once familiar and new, approachable and antagonistic. Whilst the result may be perverse – and Bridges is not the only commentator to label Browne's designs with this term – it is probably too negative an assessment to suggest that he is contemplating American decline. His contribution to Sotheby's aptly named the 'Vision of America' auction series suggests that he is more hopeful and positive.

The run-up to America's presidential election in 2024 even showed him to be protective of America. During New York Fashion Week in September, Anna Wintour, editor-in-chief of US *Vogue*, led a march and rally in the city's Herald Square to encourage Americans to vote for their next president. This 'unprecedented' event was organised by *Vogue* and CFDA, which Browne chairs.[56] Wintour was joined by more than 1,000 people, including fashion models, designers and influencers. Thom Browne was prominently among them.

Dressed identically in white T-shirts printed with the slogan 'Fashion for our Future', participants called for Americans to engage in the democratic process to elect their next president. The CFDA described the event as 'non-partisan', but the reality was different.[57] In July, *Vogue* had publicly endorsed Democratic candidate Kamala Harris for president, following Joe Biden's unexpected withdrawal from the race.[58] If there were any doubt about the political leanings of *Vogue* and the CFDA, the marchers were joined by the First Lady of the United States, Dr Jill Biden, who wore another of the slogan T-shirts. In a short speech, Biden spoke of her appreciation for Wintour: 'No one has shaped this industry more than you have [...] But you haven't stopped there. Now you're shaping the world. The president and I value your counsel and your friendship.'[59] Whilst these words were directed towards *Vogue*'s editor, the sentiment about world-shaping equally applies to Browne, who uses his designs, and latterly the resources of the CFDA, to champion an American-centred vision of a world that is framed by his past and desires for the future.

Chapter 3

ELIZABETHAN CLOWNS

Thom Browne's tenth womenswear collection, Spring/Summer 2014, debuted during New York Fashion Week in September 2013.[60] It provides an example of the rigour and ridiculousness that have come to define Browne's communication of his designs and brand. The collection and its runway presentation defied attempts at quick analysis, and they remain among Browne's more enigmatic designs. Some clarity becomes possible if connections with the designer's menswear collection from the same season are explored. Browne's menswear debuted nine months earlier than womenswear, during Paris Fashion Week, but the two collections share themes and motifs. Comparison of the two shows demonstrates the totality of the world that Browne has tried to create, the rigour of his conceptualisation and design, and, no less important, the discomfiture that he is prepared to impose to ensure his audiences and consumers understand both. Consequently, whilst this chapter focuses on the womenswear collection for Spring/Summer 2014, references to the season's menswear collection will be made in the pursuit of explaining the perplexing.

The forty looks of Browne's Spring/Summer womenswear collection were presented in a claustrophobic white-columned hall within the Chelsea Arts Space. Various commentators likened the set to an insane asylum. The creepy medical vibe was emphasised through props. White pills in glass jars and silver dispensing trays were placed on pedestals along either side of the runway. During the show, models doled out these counterfeit drugs to members of the audience from small pill boxes. Songs that referenced madness and melancholy formed the soundtrack, including several from *One Flew Over the Cuckoo's Nest*, a movie from 1975 set within a psychiatric hospital. Two songs by Björk – '*It's Oh So Quiet*' and '*Cvalda*' – opened and closed the show. '*It's Oh So Quiet*' begins with the Icelandic singer repeatedly shushing listeners. The sound of the artist's voice echoing around the performance space seemed an intentional act to disorientate the audience. It compounded a sense of ennui triggered by naked flickering lightbulbs that emitted an orangery-red glow, the track of several women laughing deliriously, and the suspension of headless mannequins from the ceiling. This was an incongruous setting for a collection that was loosely inspired by the sixteenth century, more specifically Elizabethan clowns.

The collection's looks were divided into two sections. The first ten models to appear were dressed wholly in white. Their tailored outfits featured designs conventionally associated with military uniforms – short-cut jackets with broad lapels, slash pockets, rows of buttons, open weave headwear that resembled berets. Anchor-shaped pins were affixed to some of the jacket lapels. From a distance, these looked like military insignia. All models wore circular metal-rimmed spectacles with black lenses. The concealment of the eyes was reminiscent of aviator sunglasses, and it conferred a menacing sense of authority on the decade of women. These were the doctors or orderlies that worked within Browne's dystopian hospital. The appearance and attitude of these models also referenced Browne's menswear collection that had been shown in Paris nine months earlier.

Across both collections, the style of the military jackets was strikingly similar. The anchor-shaped motifs that adorned several items in the womenswear collection were identical in design to those that had been worn by Browne's male models, as was their placement as insignia. The use of sunglasses to conceal the eyes and the models' expressions was also similar. The models within the menswear show had worn mirrored Aviators. The strong visual link between Browne's two seasonal collections suggests they shared an overarching concept. Nonetheless, the womenswear collection and runway possessed its own identity and influence. This was apparent in the second part of the show.

After the first ten models had walked the runway, they remained on set for the remainder of the show, as if to police the rest of the models, the audience, or both. The thirty looks that followed were more feminine. They were also more colourful. Garments were richly embroidered and, whilst predominantly white, featured hints of red, white and blue from the brand's grosgrain signature ribbon. The models also wore red, white and blue make-up. The first ten looks had narrow and simple silhouettes, defined by hobble skirts and shorts. Those that followed had expanded and more elaborate silhouettes. Protrusions from the shoulders, chest and hips, created by layers and gatherings of fabric, physically enlarged the models (Figure 3.1). Dresses with open V-neck fronts and the use of elongated collars contrasted with the buttoned-up garments of the all-in-white orderlies that had opened the show. These later garments, with their subtle references to lace collars and cuffs and the farthingale, a wide-hemmed skirt that had been fashionable for aristocratic European women during the sixteenth century, most readily signalled the Tudor influence.

The Elizabethan look was achieved through unusual materials, including latex and *papier mâché*, which created distinctive textures. In interviews, Browne explained that these materials were sufficiently stiff to morph the body into different shapes. The result was dysmorphic and an exaggeration of the models' bodies.[61] Shoulders and thighs became the sites of protruding bulges and folds that were variously smooth or heavily textured. The patchwork nature of many garments created the impression that the fabric was moving across the models' bodies, slowly enveloping and consuming them.

Figure 3.1 Female model from Thom Browne's Spring/Summer womenswear 2014 collection. Photograph by Chelsea Lauren via Getty Images.

In the case of the collection's thirty-fourth look, this seemed to be the literal case. The model's sleeved arms were crossed in front of their abdomen and appeared to be bound together, straight jacket-like, in swathes of fabric that resembled torn bandages. Their hands were completely concealed, bound within an angular, irregular form of latex and silk.

Similar techniques had been used to create the menswear collection, albeit to a less unsettling effect. The designer explained that he did not want to use undergarments to provide shape. He wanted the garments to support themselves: 'a lot of the pin tucking and the bonding of softer fabrics onto stiffer fabrics gave a lot of the development in the shapes of the clothes.'[62] This rigorous attention to technique and detail explains why various commentators thought both collections resembled *haute couture* more than ready-to-wear. Within the womenswear collection, the designer's artful contortionism was also demonstrated through the styling of jewellery. Some models walked with Elizabethan-appropriate strings of pearls that appeared to defy gravity and hang perpendicular to the wearers' bodies.

On the one hand, these playful references to the past created a sense of liberation because the shapes, colours and textures produced more personalised, characterful appearances. However, this liberty was limited. The make-up worn by the models was smudged and hinted at psychological distraction or physical torment. This idea was amplified by some of the clothes that had been finished to create the impression that they were worn and frayed. Unfastened bags dangled from the models' hands and wrists, as if they were oblivious to carrying them. Vacant expressions and oscillating head movements certainly suggested these women were not altogether sure of their surroundings.

What did the collection mean? Tim Blanks, *Business of Fashion* editor-at-large, commented wryly, '[l]et no one say Thom Browne makes things easy for his audience'.[63] There is definitely a danger – madness? – in looking too hard for meaning. Andrew Bolton was clear that he got 'Elizabethan clowns' when speaking in a post-show interview. However, in the same interview, Browne himself stated the Elizabethan motifs had 'no real reason other than I loved it and I loved the volume that I could get with that reference, the volume and the colours and the shoulders'.[64] In a subsequent conversation with *Women's Wear Daily*, the designer expressed an interest in the sinister clown but he did not elaborate on the source of his intrigue.[65]

A reconciliation between these reactions is possible if we reflect on the connections between the womenswear and menswear collections. The visual links between the garments emphasise the importance of inversion, chiefly between discipline and disorder, probity and perfidy. Within menswear, Browne achieved this by queering military uniforms and creating a confident male figure in 'not so masculine uniforms'.[66] Within womenswear, *Los Angeles Times* journalist Booth Moore questioned if the contrasts between liberation and lunacy were 'a metaphor for the female experience'.[67] Inadvertently, Tim Blanks made a connection between both collections and shows when he pondered how men and women in weakened states contemplate disorder differently:

> It's one of the cliches of [the] lunatic asylum
> [...] that men think they're Napoleon.
> I wonder if women think they're Elizabeth I.[68]

In essence, this is what Browne's collections and shows appeared to be doing. By demonstrating inversion to a heightened, ridiculous, degree, he drew attention to the precarity of 'western' social structures and the concepts that underpin them, which are often demonstrated and maintained through clothing. The use of garments to define social positions – gender, sex and status above all – is readily apparent in the past. During the Elizabethan period, sumptuary legislation still attempted to restrict the colours, quantities and quality of materials that people wore based on social hierarchy. From the past and into the present, the idea of clothing demarcating social position, and order, is most readily apparent in uniforms, perhaps especially those worn by the military.

On one level, Browne's womenswear collection asserts the need for clothing to convey discipline and rigour in the maintenance of social order. However, the staging of the catwalk show emphasises how the existence of control is always remarkably close to chaos. In this sense, he seems to hint at the idea that unbridled fun and outright fantasy are not diametrically opposed to discipline, but closely related to it. The one feeds off, and even passes into and enhances, the other. To varying degrees, the theme of control and chaos frames the stories that Browne fashions through his collections and narrates through his runway shows.

Chapter 4

THOM'S ARK

Thom Browne's menswear and womenswear collection for Fall and Winter 2020 were shown together during Paris Fashion Week within the city's *L'Ecole des Beaux Arts*. The runway show was a loose interpretation of the Old Testament Biblical story of Noah's Ark. It imagined the period after the epic flood and depicted animals and humans, who walked two-by-two, leaving their protective shelter and looking towards the future.

The runway was a snowscape dotted with white-stemmed leafless birch trees and conifers. At either end, a free-standing wooden frame housed a pair of closed panelled doors, each fitted with a large round brass handle. The presentation began with a procession of eight models, each of whom wore a zoomorphic head covering decorated in the colours of the brand's grosgrain ribbon (red, white and blue) – giraffe, rhinoceros, lion, deer, elephant, hippopotamus, zebra and pig. The animalesque models all wore the same outfit: blazer, skirt, mid-torso vest resembling a corset, shirt and tie. Except for the solid white shirt, the models' garments were a playful riot of miss-matched stripes of varying thickness in the brand's signature colours (red–white–blue).

As the models entered, one by one, the score of '*Carnival of the Animals*' by Camille Saint-Saens played. In Browne's interpretation of the animal kingdom, the lion was not the king of beasts. The giraffe played the part of orchestrator and gyrated and swayed as they completed a circuit of the runway, leading the other models, who came to position themselves around its perimeter (Figure 4.1). The models who wore the hippopotamus and lion masks, respectively, stood either side of the runway's first set of doors. Browne has said this portal represented the past. The models who wore the zebra and pig masks, respectively, stood either side of the doors at the end of the runway. Browne has said this opening represented the future.[69] The four remaining models stood among the seated audience and faced the runway. Their position blurred the boundary between the romance of Browne's world and the reality of the show's commerciality. Shortly after the show's third minute, the models flanking the doors reached to open them. The main part of the performance began as pairs of models wearing the collection's remaining thirty-three looks appeared on the runway. Each pair showed the male and female variants of one look, although Browne was clear that he wanted ambiguity to surround the models' sex and gender.[70] Coats – heavy three-quarter length, puffer and voluminously

Figure 4.1 Look 1 from Thom Browne's Fall/Winter 2020/2021 collection. Photograph by Victor Virgile/Gamma-Rapho via Getty Images.

sleeved – dominated the collection, which was more conventionally tailored. There were some exceptions. Look thirty-three provided a more unconventional interpretation of a suit jacket. The double-breasted garment looked like it was in the process of sliding down the models' bodies. It appeared to have slipped off their left shoulder and was attached, just barely, to their right thigh. This studied dishevelment, which only emphasised Browne's skill in perfecting the balance of a tailored jacket, appeared all the greater because the two panels of the jacket were cut from cloths of contrasting patterns. Mis-aligned as these garments were, they presented a more coherent and recognisable appearance than look twenty, which played with the idea of inversion. A pair of grey flannel trousers was worn as a halter neck top and a navy jacket and white shirt were attached to the front of a garment that resembled a hobble skirt.

The final model pairing to walk the runway had a large grey snake draped across their shoulders (Figure 4.2). The extent to which this was conceived as a comment on another Biblical story, and the tempting of Eve in the Garden of Eden by a snake, is unclear. For the finale, models returned to the catwalk in pairs that mixed sexes and looks. The officiating giraffe followed the models in making a final circuit of the runway. As they walked to leave the runway, they were followed by the animal bystanders. The couple who had stood as sentinels at the door symbolizing the past closed it before they, too, disappeared from view.

Figure 4.2 Look 41 from Thom Browne's Fall/Winter 2020/2021 collection. Photograph by Victor Virgile/Gamma-Rapho via Getty Images.

The discussion of *Thom Browne*'s womenswear collection for Spring/Summer 2014 in Chapter 3 emphasised the relationship between control and chaos within the designs and presentations of his work. In an interview with *AnOther* magazine about his Fall and Winter 2020 show, Browne clarified this linkage. He explained that '[a] collection always starts from proportion – by thinking about how I can play with proportions in a different way, in a way that will make the collection evolve.'[71] The discipline and control that is achieved through Browne's distinctive tailoring is played with – elaborated upon, reinterpreted, stretched – to create something that is simultaneously recognisable and new. Browne uses the verb 'to push' to explain how he intentionally collides concepts. In the case of the Fall and Winter collection, he wanted to push 'strong feminine ideas into the men's collection and strong masculine ideas into the women's collection [...] The most interesting idea with this collection was the notion of the looks being pushed to a point where you really didn't know who was the guy and who was the girl.'

An emphasis on exaggeration within fashion design to facilitate expression has been explored by fashion scholars Adam Geczy and Vicki Karaminas, who acknowledge the importance of dress as 'a means of registration and difference'. They go further, however, and define critical fashion practice as a particular form of fashion where 'design approaches and staging (catwalk)' are conspicuously 'stretched' and 'exaggerated' through 'extension' and the 'unconventional'.[72] They argue that these characteristics imbue designs with 'critical qualities formerly afforded by art', a label that includes literature and music. Geczy and Karaminas assert that art's criticality decreased in inverse correlation to its growing popularity between the nineteenth and twentieth centuries, 'because it sought accountability in the open market and became subject to the popular opinion that it believed it could alter'.[73] The critical fashion practice they describe does not exist in the majority of clothing, which is characterised by useful and unobtrusive garments, but where it does exist, there is 'a discernible space where cultural critique exists that is as searching and as lasting as that found in good works of art'.[74]

Browne's explicit focus on gender within this collection, or more specifically, the blurring of it, was a response to 'the times we're living [in]'. His desire for 'escape and fantasy' is similarly influenced by present concerns. Nonetheless, the extent to which he was seeking to make a sustained and critical comment on centuries-old gender binaries is unclear. He is frank that 'sometimes my ideas aren't as intellectually thought-out as some people think'.[75] Reflecting on the fact that he is easily bored, Browne explains that he loves 'taking really simple ideas and putting them in front of people'. He is, however, interested in how his designs might be 'interpreted in a deeper way' by others.[76] The reticence, even reluctance, that Browne evinces about the epistemological merits of his collections and shows is likely a reflection of the close connection he has to his brand. To him, his designs may not appear intellectually meritorious because they seem like offshoots of his character and preoccupations, much like the rest of his brand.

This point can be explored further by thinking about the pair of doors that stood at either end of the runway. Browne's explanation that these conspicuous props represented the past and future, respectively, appeared within a film interview that aired after the event.[77] Consequently, it is doubtful the live audience interpreted the doors as anything other than dramatic cues to signal the commencement and conclusion of the show. This ambiguity raises at least two queries, which are applicable to all the designer's catwalk presentations. First, it is probable that there was a detachment between what the live audience thought they had seen and what Browne knew was happening. Second, it sparks consideration of how far Browne presents ideas in his shows for personal rumination and enjoyment or whether he is genuinely committed to spark discussion among his audiences and fashion reporters. The symbiotic relationship that Browne has with his brand makes both assessments probable. His deep immersion in the world he has created may lead him to think that his ideas are conveyed more clearly than is the case. Browne's inclination to downplay his ideas, which he presumably considers obvious or commonsensical because of his familiarity with them, could be the cause of this oversight.

Whatever the reality, the layering of different stories that Browne refers to in an interview with journalist Alexander Fury demonstrates that this creative process is more than whimsy. However subconsciously, he is engaging with Georges Didi-Huberman's concept of anachronistic comparison (Chapter 2) and the tensions and opportunities that arise when different chronologies, and the ideas that defined them, are collided together.[78]

Conceptually, Browne is layering the Old Testament story of Noah's ark and its binary interpretation of gender, with a contemporary recognition that gender is a construct existing across a spectrum. Physically, he is layering traditional tailoring practices with his own personal practices. These are framed by 'American references' that focus on the preppie aesthetic. Motifs that allude to mid-twentieth century America include the brand's signature grosgrain, which provides the colourway for striped neckwear and blazers, coats trimmed with contrasting colours, and footwear that resembles moccasins. The recurrence of American symbols provides a visual coherence to Browne's collection, irrespective of how deeply they are understood by audiences. They manifest the juxtaposition between control and chaos, or 'fantasy' as he describes it.[79] Fundamentally, they underscore the autobiographical nature of Browne's work, which may at once diminish his awareness of its wider relevance and his ability to clearly articulate it.

There are clear limits to the cultural connectivity of Browne's designs. A personal insistence that his inspiration is simple, often playful, and rooted within America, emphasises the figurative boundaries of the Brownean world. Focus on the suit and tailoring defines its physical boundaries. These perimeters confirm Browne's outlook as thoroughly 'western'-centric. This is readily apparent through the collection's references to Catholicism. The Old Testament story of the flood is a framing device, and the show's final pairing seems to make a pointed reference to the transgression of Adam and Eve. Appropriation of Catholic motifs by 'western' fashion designers has long become commonplace. The *Heavenly Bodies: Fashioning the Catholic Imagination* exhibition that was organised by the Costume Institute of the Metropolitan Museum of Art, New York, in 2018, asserted the cultural dominance and legitimacy of Catholicism and the precarity of other global faiths. Commentary about the exhibition established that Catholic imagery is so suffuse within 'western' culture that the Church is 'fair game' for fashion designers to use as they choose. This contrasts with other faiths, notably Islam and Judaism, where criticisms of cultural appropriation have dogged designers using their sacred symbolism for secular purposes.[80] The use of Catholic motifs may be especially personal for Browne, who continued his education at the Catholic University of Notre Dame, following in the footsteps of his father and sister.

The final paired look of the collection, which took zoomorphic inspiration from the serpent, may support this point (Figure 4.2). Look forty-one was at one with the thirty-two looks that had come before. The male and female models were identically dressed, save for their varying proportions. The uppermost part of their ensemble was inspired by a morning coat. The lower part was an ankle-length skirt with a three-quarter split running vertically up the front. Both garments were mid-grey, but cut from different cloths. The jacket was embellished with ruching and metallic threads. The skirt was fashioned from two contrasting pieces of grey tweed. The grid pattern on one of the panels was approximately three times the size of that on the other. Both garments were lined with a vertically striped cloth in the colours of the *Thom Browne* grosgrain label (red–white–navy). The under layer was an interpretation of a white shirt. The garment had a crew-neck with a penny collar detail affixed as decoration. A pale grey placket with four white buttons was decorated with diagonally striped bands in red–white–navy. Unfolded French cuffs protruded from the sleeves of the jacket, framing the wearer's black-gloved hands. The lower third of the shirt was tucked into a vertically banded cummerbund with thick stripes of pale and mid-grey and narrow white stripes. The models' legs were uncovered. They wore thick, long grey socks that were bundled around their shins. The socks were patterned with a tonal grey argyle design that was interspersed with a band of four horizontal white stripes above the mid-section. The models wore white laced boots of black and white leather. The footwear had no vamp, so the argyle pattern of the socks was fully visible from the front. Briefly sketched, the look encapsulates the juxtaposition of control and fantasy.

This is emphasised by Browne's playful use of the snake, which appeared at three points within the design. First, a rudimentary serpent outline was embellished at regular intervals across the skirt. Second, a coiled serpent in black leather, its forked tongue the *Thom Browne* grosgrain label, was fashioned into an impractical bag that each model carried in hands. Third, a larger serpent, draped across the models' shoulders and wrapped between their facing hands, completed the look. The tail of this snake terminated with three stripes in the colours of the *Thom Browne* grosgrain label, red–white–navy. This was mirrored by the snake's forked-tongue, which, like the bag, was fashioned from a length of striped material in red–white–navy.

The snake, which precipitated Original Sin and the Fall of Man, represents corruption and deception. It seems a dicey choice for a luxury fashion brand to conjure with, particularly because the animal bags, which vary in price from $1,809 to $3,550 (£1,350–£4,440), could be said to reflect humankind's propensity to sin. The bags surely represent at least five of the cardinal sins: envy, gluttony, greed, lust and pride. This may have been the point. It was a statement, less to chastise would-be consumers, but to refute Catholicism's stringent, unrealistic expectations. Speaking in 2022, Browne said that he references his Catholic upbringing 'all the time, whether directly or indirectly. I think there's something interesting and fun about subverting it and giving it to people in an inappropriate way'.[81]

The critical tone he adopts towards Catholicism is also apparent in the decision to include a near life-size model of a snake. The position of the snake, which physically connects the bodies of the male and female bodies, seems to be a literal manifestation of Browne's desire to 'push' the sexes into each other. Superficially, the snake is a non-binary creature because it possesses, to the untrained eye, no obvious indication of its sex. It is arguably the perfect animal to demonstrate, and conclude, Browne's insistence that gendered differences are social constructs. If this interpretation is accepted, the Christian connotations of the snake are turned upside down. Within the Old Testament story, the snake emphasised the gendered gulf between Man and Woman. Within Browne's telling, the snake literally bridges this gap. Its appearance at the end of the catwalk seems to dare onlookers and subsequent commentators to argue that a binary gendered division exists considering the collection they have just seen.

If Browne were seeking to lampoon the Catholic Church, he was doing it with an inside perspective, drawing upon his Catholic upbringing within the United States. He was also making his argument through expensive clothing and dress accessories that are unaffordable to most people. Critical as it may have been, his argument was at least partially framed by the privilege and cultural myopia he sought to challenge. Moreover, through his model pairings, which deliberately placed a man and woman together, his presentation arguably did as much to buttress as blast a gendered division that the 'western' fashion industry has long maintained.[82] The collection was racially diverse, however. Fifteen of the model pairings were white (45%), twelve were black (36%), six were mixed (18%), where one of the couple was black and one was white. Consequently, it could be said that Browne's collection was making a decisive effort to disrupt attitudes and ideologies that the 'western' fashion industry has galvanised since its development during the eighteenth and nineteenth centuries. The ability of Browne's collection to do this is linked to its juxtaposition of control and fantasy, because it is through the conjoined presentation of the serious and silly that contradictions and incongruities within dominant attitudes and behaviours are surfaced for critique, because their veneer of taken-for-grantedness is shattered. However, the extent to which people beyond Browne can fully engage and understand the complex ideas that a collection like this presents is unclear. Here, his world is as enigmatic as it appears enticing.

Chapter 5

THE LITTLE PRINCE

Thom Browne's menswear and womenswear collection for Fall 2023 was shown during New York Fashion Week on Valentine's Day.[83] The timing was probably coincidental, but themes within the catwalk presentation were appropriate for a festivity celebrating love and companionship. The Shed, a futuristic-looking adaptable arts space within Hudson Yards, was transformed into a fantastical timepiece as the designer presented his sixty-two piece collection in a runway show inspired by Antoine de Saint-Exupéry's *Le Petit Prince* (*The Little Prince*). First published in 1943, in French and English, the novella is ostensibly for children, but is beloved by people of all ages. It has been translated into over 500 languages because of the universality of its themes, which include imagination, friendship and loneliness. The meandering story recounts the journey of an inquisitive space-travelling adolescent, resident of an asteroid called B-162 that has three volcanoes (two

active, one extinct), an infestation of baobab, a fast-growing
weed and a vain, talking rose that he loves and tenders. The
Little Prince visits six asteroids – identified by the numbers
325, 326, 327, 328, 329 and 330 – before appearing on
Earth in Africa's Sahara Desert. Within this isolated, barren
landscape, the youth meets the story's pilot-cum-narrator,
who had crash-landed before him. The traveller, who is nick-
named the 'Little Prince' by the pilot, recounts his galactic
travels as the aviator works to repair his aircraft before the
pair succumb to dehydration. Browne's decision to focus on
this eighty-year old story has been linked to Meghan Sullivan,
Wilsey Family College Professor of Philosophy at his *alma mater*
the University Notre Dame, who quoted the story in a meeting
with the designer. During Spring 2023, Sullivan co-taught a
one-credit course on Thom Browne with colleague and art
historian Professor Michael Schreffler, 'Strong Suits: The Art,
Philosophy, and Business of Thom Browne'.[84]

The catwalk that brought the Little Prince's universe to life
was circular and resembled the face of an analogue clock.[85]
Arabic numbers and markers for seconds and minutes were
projected around the outer edge of circle, which was brightly
lit. The centre was dimly lit. In place of clock hands, a full-size
biplane fashioned from translucent white paper was cushioned
in a softly mounded dune of ivory coloured sand. The scene
depicted the crash site of the story's unnamed narrator. Sand,
apparently eight tonnes of it, covered the entirety of the circular
catwalk and glinted in the studio lights.[86] The cavernous interior

of the Shed was painted black, presumably to resemble space. Spheres and five-pointed stars, created from the same material as the biplane, were suspended from an unseen ceiling. The celestial objects alluded to the galaxy through which the Little Prince had travelled. The audience, who were seated around the catwalk in three rows, were largely unseen.

The ensuing show, which lasted for over thirty minutes, was one of Browne's longest, and most creative. Nonetheless, there were connections to his previous catwalk presentations, making this more a difference of degree than kind. A dominant theme was monotony and routine. In part, this was evidenced by the duration of the show, which began forty minutes after its scheduled start because of the late-arriving singer Erykah Badu. Other celebrities in attendance, of which there were many – Penn Badgley, Whoopie Goldberg, Queen Latifah, Lil Nas X and Christine Baranski – had arrived punctually. On many previous occasions, Browne has used the slow passage of time to urge people to pause and question their surroundings. The sound of a ticking clock, which could be heard throughout, provided a more direct, even wearying, indication of the designer's interest in order and the extent to which he seeks to disrupt contemporary 'western' assumptions about time. Like many of his previous shows, there was a sense that Browne delighted in the clock's rhythmic beat to indicate linear progression and discipline, what Caroline Evans and Alessandra Vaccari have termed 'industrial time'.[87] Simultaneously, he appeared to wilfully defy time as the constant ticking heightened the audience's awareness of their enforced inactivity. For over thirty minutes, they were prevented from doing anything constructive.

The manipulation of time emphasised Browne's strong narrative voice, which has gradually increased throughout all his runway shows. Typically, through written prompts on show invitations or notes, Browne guides the audience on how they should interpret his work and see it through his eyes.[88] Within the Shed, an unseen female narrator provided audible prompts for the audience. The statements included verbatim and abridged passages from Saint-Exupéry's text.

The show commenced with the Little Prince, played by a female model, meandering the perimeter of the catwalk. Wearing 'grey flannel tweed tailoring over a dress embroidered with gold bullion baobab roots', s/he was joined by a black female model, who represented the pilot.[89] The aviator's ensemble comprised 'beading, fringe, and earthy tulle'.[90] Their paisley suit and platform astronaut boots showed influences of American football with its voluminous sleeves and trousers that resembled shoulder and shin padding. After spotting each other, the pair conversed inaudibly. Approximately three minutes later, they were joined by seven white male models who were introduced by the narrator as a king ('a very vain man'), a drunkard, a lamp-lighter, a businessman and a geographer. The septet represented characters from each of the asteroids the Little Prince had visited before his arrival on Earth (Figure 5.1). Their dress was inspired by the original drawings

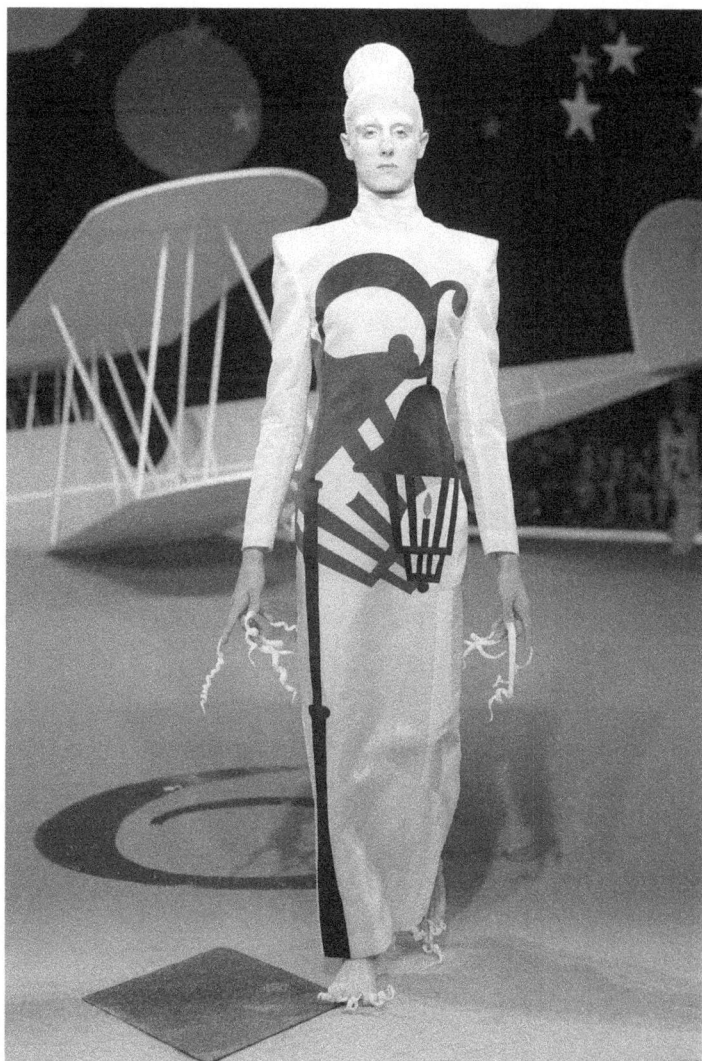

Figure 5.1 Look 7 from Thom Browne's Fall/Winter 2023 collection. Photograph by Giovanni Giannoni/WWD via Getty Images.

that Saint-Exupéry created for his story's first publication. They wore partially translucent white full-sleeved ankle-length gowns with turtlenecks. Vertical rows of buttons along the rear of the sleeves and back of the gown provided structural decoration. The front of the gowns were decorated with motifs in black, blue, red and yellow that identified the characters. For example, the gown of the lamp-lighter featured a lamp post and the gown of the drunkard included a bottle of wine and drinking glass. Browne's embellishment was to give the men long, curled white nails that were affixed to their fingers and toes designed by Juan Alvear.

The models entered the catwalk from behind the pilot's plane near the number '12' on the clock face. They walked clockwise, completing a full circuit of the circle before stopping at regular intervals to form a perimeter around the biplane. The men remained here, flexing their elongated fingernails throughout the show. After approximately seven minutes, the first models wearing Browne's 2023 Fall collection appeared. They entered the catwalk at '12' and retraced the footsteps of the planetary ambassadors until reaching the number '4' of the clockface. At this point, they turned towards the centre of the circle. Upon reaching the plane, the models changed direction again and walked towards '6', and what was ostensibly the front of the runway. From here, they completed their circuit of the catwalk and followed the remaining numbers along its edge back to '12'.

The collection was divided in three parts. The first, 'the clocks', included looks 1–24; the second, looks 25–30; the third, 'the asteroids', looks 31–52.[91] Each section possessed a loose visual coherence. The preppie influence was clear throughout. The first focused on tweed overcoats, with atypically wide shoulders. Models carried black leather bags of various styles decorated with a round gold-coloured clock face. The models' footwear continued the chronological theme. The heel of their pointed platform shoes was formed into a round clock face, making them as visually striking as they were physically cumbersome. Over their heads the models wore a gold-coloured metal lattice. The significance of this detail and connection to Saint-Exupéry's story was unclear.

The second section, which comprised six looks, was influenced by one of the more significant passages within *The Little Prince*, which occurs when the young boy meets and converses with a wild fox. Through their conversation, the pair dwell on the effort required to nurture friendship and the extent to which companionship enriches a person's life. The dialogue prompts the Little Prince to reflect on his relationship with the rose on his asteroid, and the values he derives from her presence. Within the frame of the story, the exchange between boy and fox emphasises the importance of interpersonal connections and self-reflection, which most adults are said to overlook.

This part of the catwalk show began with the appearance of a female model, who wore a waist-length matte sequin jacket and skirt over a grey hand pulled chiffon tweed dress. The rear of their bustier-style dress was decorated with an intarsia paisley bow. The model represented an elephant. Their platted blonde hair was styled to create the impression of a trunk and the outline of two droopy ears. The only elephant to appear in *The Little Prince* is that created by the narrator-cum-pilot in 'Drawing Number One'. This *trompe l'oeil* illustration depicts a boa constrictor digesting an elephant. In two dimensions, most adults apparently saw the illustration as nothing but a hat and criticised the pilot's creativity and imaginative talent, urging him to give up drawing and focus on subjects with more obvious utility, like 'geography, history, arithmetic, and grammar'.[92] The model carried a realisation of the narrator's drawing in the form of a black leather bag. Browne's bag was admittedly less abstract. The elephant's tusks were depicted in white, and the snake's forked tongue was fashioned from the brand's grosgrain ribbon, as it had been when a snake featured in his Fall and Winter 2020 collection.[93] The decision to reference Drawing Number One at this point in the catwalk presentation helped to establish a fundamental point within the story of the Little Prince – and Browne's world – about the importance of perceiving more than is readily apparent.

This point is emphasised by the four male models who appeared next. They each wore a wide-shouldered gown with a turtleneck, which resembled the dress of the planetary ambassadors, and had similar, cone-shaped hairstyles. The sombre-looking quartet presumably represented the humans that are admonished by the fox for having no time to understand anything:

They buy things all ready made at the shops. But there is no shop anywhere where one can buy friendship, and so men have no friends any more.[94]

To underscore this judgement, the first of the four men carried a black leather bag in the shape of a rose. This is a reference to the solitary flower the Little Prince cared for on his asteroid. It is only through his conversation with the fox that the youth comes to appreciate the personal significance of this relationship. He had felt sad, even cheated, upon seeing multiple roses on Earth and allowing himself to believe that his rose on B-162 was merely one other. The fox helps the Little Prince to realise that the rose he knows is unique because of the experiences they alone have shared.

The final model to appear in this section, a female, was conceived to represent the fox. The model's reddish-brown hair had been styled to form two pointed ears. Their degrade beaded dress with silk-cotton fringe and Swarovski crystals was similarly coloured. Its texture resembled fur. Cosmetics applied to the model's face heightened their animalesque appearance through the suggestion of whiskers and fangs. In their left hand, the model carried a black leather bag in the shape of a fox. As the model walked, the show's narrator read from Saint-Exupéry's story:

It's quite simple. One sees clearly only with the heart. Anything essential is invisible to the eyes.[95]

The second section of Browne's show was something of an interpolation. The clothes and models' appearance served the story the designer wished to tell. The final segment of the show, which comprised looks 31–52, was more obviously connected to Browne's previous catwalks and collections. It included ensembles fashioned from de-constructed tailoring – skirts made from suit jackets and shirts, jackets turned inside-out and ties used as belts. The pronounced creativity of this section and abstract silhouettes led two journalists to suggest the models represented children.[96] This reading is plausible and suitably heartfelt, and Browne had explained that 'the more conceptual tailoring meant the kids actually saw things as more interesting', but notes accompanying the show clarify that the models in this segment represented asteroids.[97] The tell-tale clue was provided by the models' head coverings. More elaborate than the metallic meshes worn by models in the show's first segment, these creations resembled de-constructed crowns. The headwear comprised twisted vertical rods of a gold-coloured metal that were supported by a flexible woven lattice. The show notes explained that these represented the baobab plants on the Little Prince's asteroid. The back of each of the headpieces was individually numbered. *The Little Prince* is a story with many numerical references – the businessman who is continuously counting; the 1440 sunsets of the lamp-lighter's planet; the Geographer's quantitative survey of the Earth; the days the Little Prince remains on Earth. In this case, the numbers appear to have designated individual asteroids.

After the twenty-three models had completed their walk in their buckled platform astronaut boots, a female model entered the catwalk space at the number '8' on the clockface. They personified the story's snake, a creature 'that take[s] just thirty seconds to bring [...] life to an end'.[98] Within Saint-Exupéry's story, the snake appears on the one-year anniversary of the Little Prince's arrival on Earth. It is also his last day because the snake bites the boy. This section of the story is ambiguous, but the implication is that the venomous bite proves fatal. The model/snake, who was accompanied by a rattling sound as they walked the runway counterclockwise, wore a slim-fitting dress. Across the front of their garment, black, grey and white stacked sequins depicted a rudimentary anatomical design. Viewed from the side and rear, the patterns on the dress resembled scales. Sleeves that extended to the floor hung behind the model as she walked, emphasising the impression of slithering. Their hairstyle continued the serpent theme. Two strands of platted hair – perhaps representing the snake's tail or forked tongue – were positioned so that one coiled behind the model's head and under the left side of their chin. The other strand wrapped around the right of their head and across their forehead. The model/snake approached the Little Prince, and circled 'him'. Any bite or violent exchange was omitted, as it is in Saint-Exupéry's story. The model then retraced their steps and walked out of the catwalk space. The lights darkened and a spotlight focused on the Little Prince, who removed their jacket, reclined and appeared to fall asleep. Simultaneously,

American model Precious Lee entered the catwalk at '12' on
the clockface. Lee personified an angel, a character that does
not appear in Saint-Exupéry's story.[99] Lee wore a white lace-up
tweed dress with deconstructed tailoring and gathered sheer
silk stole with pearls. The skirt and its train were fashioned
from suit jackets, some of which were turned inside-out. As Lee
walked, the narrator read an extract of the Little Prince's final
words to the pilot. The youth sought to reassure the aviator that
he would live on after his departure from Earth. Their year-
long experience together would be immortalised in the celestial
memories of the stars:

> People have stars, but they aren't all the same. For
> travellers, the stars are guides; for other people, they're
> nothing but tiny lights; and for still others, for scholars,
> they're problems. But all those stars are silent stars. You,
> though, you'll have stars like nobody else.[100]

The catwalk was suffused in a warm light as Lee reached the
Little Prince. Rousing, and standing, the 'boy' proceeded to
walk around the circular space. Simultaneously, the show's
models returned for their final runway walk in gendered pairs,
a characteristic of Browne's shows. They were accompanied by
the song 'You'll Never Walk Alone' from the Broadway musical
'Carousel'. The Little Prince and angel followed the models off
the stage. Before leaving, s/he waved to the audience. As the
lighting of the catwalk darkened, and the audience began their

applause, Browne appeared to receive their applause clutching a heart-shaped box, presumably of chocolates, that he presented to his partner, Andrew Bolton, a personal and fitting touch for Valentine's Day.

The show was reviewed positively by many fashion commentators. Vanessa Friedman, fashion director and chief fashion critic for *The New York Times*, praised Browne's ability to combine 'minimal lines and maximal fabrication [...] feeling and functionality'.[101] Other reviewers described the show variously as 'fantastical'[102] and 'heartfelt'[103]. Accounts suggest Browne's message was broadly understood. Talking after the show, he explained that his presentation was about 'the adults who don't understand anything and the kids who understand everything [...] It's so important to create a fantasy that makes the world so much more interesting to live with.'[104] For him, 'the shows are pure creativity. I don't think about business and commerce at all. It's all about ideas and concepts. That part of it is important, because it does create such a fantastical view of the story I'm telling.'[105]

Browne's ability to unleash the power of sartorial storytelling was considered important for this collection because it was his first as Chair of the Confederation of Fashion Designers of America.[106] Recognising the influence of preppie and sport within the clothing designs, Kristen Batemen, writing for *W* Magazine, claimed the designer 'set the tone for American fashion' by moving away from the pronounced commerciality of New York Fashion Week.[107] Friedman made a similar argument. Referring to Browne as 'America's great fashion ideologue', she described him as 'an apostle for the importance of imagination', because he understood the role of emotion in identity-building, which was as important for his eponymous brand as the American fashion industry.[108] Friedman suggested that Browne's emotional sensibility, paired with the technical accomplishment of his 'new kind of tailoring', meant he was responsible for a theorising that is rarely associated with American designers, namely, that '[w]hat you put on your outside should, and does, change how you feel on your inside.'[109]

These verdicts seemed right in parts and insufficient in sum. The suggestion that the collection marked a 'homecoming' and 'a new theory of American fashion' seems misplaced because inspiration came from a French-authored story whose themes transcend continents as much chronologies. Moreover, if Browne were advocating the theory attributed to him, it was unoriginal. The idea that dress empowers people has become an axiom of 'western' studies of human clothing and appearance. European and American scholars have explained the commercial and cultural significance of fashion by conflating character and appearance since at least the nineteenth century. In so doing, they drew upon a historical tradition, which was not unique to Europe or the United States, that securely documents connections between people's clothed appearance and their social identity from the eighth century. One of the more strident, and cynical, declarations of the connections that exist between character, self-perception and clothing was made by an American, economist Thorstein Veblen. In the final year of the nineteenth century, Veblen published *The Theory of The Leisure Class*. His survey of 'western' consumption patterns remains among the most influential to examine the motivations and meanings of contemporary dress. One of the more pernicious and persistent sentiments from Veblen's text is the 'requirement of expensiveness'. He (in)famously asserted that 'without reflection or analysis, we feel that what is inexpensive is unworthy. "A cheap coat makes a cheap man." "Cheap and nasty" is recognized to hold true in dress with even less mitigation than in other lines of consumption.'[110]

Whilst the price of *Thom Browne* products gives credence to the continuing influence of Veblen's ideas, analyses of his Fall 2023 collection were on surer ground when they emphasised the importance of the values that underscored its creation. The designer's insistence that his designs are personal and wholly divorced from commercial considerations suggests that any theory he espouses is likely to be the inversion of that suggested by Friedman, namely, that how you feel should – and does – change what you put on outside. A paradox that defines Browne's world is the fact that its values only become apparent through its exquisite materiality. Superficially, the materially gives credence to Friedman's assessment. However, as many details within the presentation of the Fall collection passed unnoticed by commentators – which is equally true of previous shows – it is reasonable to suggest that the role of materiality within his work is not fully grasped. If Browne were philosophising through his Fall collection, his designs seem to form part of his methodology. Prompting reflection, his garments are the means to realise the values he champions, rather than their full embodiment and end. Any attribution of theory or philosophy to Browne's work needs to be made cautiously because, contrary to Friedman's pronouncement, the designer would doubtless not see himself as an ideologue, nor would he want to. Nonetheless, his engagement with Saint-Exupéry's story provides a counter to remarks that his shows are often without deeper meaning.

Chapter 6

HAUTE COUTURE

On 3 July 2023, Thom Browne returned to *Palais Garnier*, Paris, to present his debut *haute couture* collection. The opera house had provided the backdrop for his 2023 Spring/ Summer womenswear collection nine months previously in October 2022. The show invitation, which asked guests to '… PLEASE WEAR YOUR BEST GREY … ', may have seemed a predictable request from a brand and designer known for monotone mastery, but a return did not mean more of the same.[111] For a start, the 300 guests entered the *Palais* from its original entrance, which is situated behind the stage and at what would now present as the rear of the building. The back-to-front positioning was emphasised by the construction of Browne's catwalk, which seated guests on the stage, under lighting and other rigging that would normally be concealed. Surprising, even disorientating audiences has become a hallmark of Browne's shows, and something of a characteristic contradiction of the designer himself, who can claim that he wants 'people to feel like they're part of what I do' and assert that they should 'either love or hate what I do', within a single interview.[112] Another indication that guests should expect the unexpected, or rather, for Browne to be Browne, was provided by a rolled slip of paper, tied with the brand's red–white–blue ribbon and placed on their seats. The message on the scroll read: 'A bird in the hand is worth two in the bush'. This proverb originates in the Old Testament Biblical book of *Ecclesiastes*, but it is generally understood as a caution against envy and greed because the idea of possessing more can never be as valuable as acknowledging what has already been obtained. A message of restraint and reflection may seem odd at the start of an *haute couture* presentation, but this was not a typical show, even for Browne.

When the curtain lifted at the start of the show, the gaze of guests was returned by a phalanx of 2002 people. Occupying the fixed seats of the *Palais Garnier*, which the audience may rightly have expected to be theirs, were a series of identical cardboard models, white and androgynous in appearance, who wore signature *Thom Browne* tailoring, sunglasses and slicked hair. The sight was accompanied by simulated applause and cheers. No such response was provided by the sentient audience, who were seated either side of a T-shaped runway, at the top of which were more lifeless props. In this case, a flock of pigeons. This curious detail, which extended to include pigeons placed around the guests' seating, provided a clue that the set was a train station concourse. Above the audience hung a large grey bell banded with the *Thom Browne* red–white–blue stripes, to emphasise the related theme of time.

The thirty-three-minute presentation, Browne's longest at the time, began when two white male models, dressed in identical grey branded skirt suits and sunglasses, entered the catwalk from opposite sides carrying pebbled leather suitcases, all mid-grey, in varying shapes and sizes. The models-cum-porters carried the luggage to the middle of the runway, where they left it to occupy positions at the runway's furthest edge. They retained their sentry-like posts for much of the show. Model Alek Wek appeared next, walking onto the catwalk from among the *Palais Garnier*'s fixed seating. Dressed in a *Thom Browne* mid-grey three-piece suit with three-quarter length trousers and skirt, Wek's face was framed by a matching cloth that she wore around her head. The model was greeted by more simulated applause when she stood at the top of the catwalk. After walking its length, she re-traced her steps to the bundled luggage. She seated herself on one of the largest cases and remained there until the finale of the show, occasionally interacting with the cloth she clutched her in hands.

As Wek arranged her clothing around her, a white male model dressed to resemble a pigeon emerged on the runway behind her, accompanied by cooing sounds (Figure 6.1). The model's grey ensemble involved deconstructed tailoring, but bore a close resemblance to a fancy dress costume. A single-button coat had been fashioned into a skirt, its shoulders repurposed to give the

Figure 6.1 Look 3 (worn by Alex Wek) and Look 4 from Thom Browne's *haute couture* Fall/Winter 2023 collection. Photograph by Thierry Chesnot via Getty Images.

impression of a pannier. The upper part of the garment was embellished with feathers. The model's headpiece reflected the idea of (de)construction. The left side provided a realistic three-dimensional depiction of a grey pigeon. By contrast, the right side was abstract, with the pigeon's head depicted only in outline. The model meandered aimlessly and artfully around Wek, who seemed oblivious, before exiting the runway from the left. He was the first of two pigeon-models to appear during the show.

No sooner had this pigeon flown, a black female model, who resembled a bell, appeared from the right of the runway. The model's garment was conceptual. Costume might be a more accurate term to describe it. The silhouette of the dress was A-line. Shoulders were sloped, and sleeves were bulbous. The front and rear of the woollen tweed and seersucker tulle garment, which was hemmed with pearls, employed *trompe l'oeils* effects. For whilst it looked like the model was wearing a suit and coat, these were two-dimensional cut-outs in the shape of jacket and overcoat that had been attached to the dress, almost like panels. The model wore a cloche-shaped headpiece that covered two-thirds of their upper face. Round holes in the base of the hat enabled them to see. A single brass bell was affixed to the rear of each of the model's stiletto platform shoes on a coiled brass rod. They chimed as the model walked, carefully. In all, twelve bell-models appeared throughout the show, their entry on the runway presaged by a chiming sound. Initially, they appeared at regular intervals, after every third model. After the appearance of the sixth bell-model, the sequence changed to an appearance after every third or fourth model. These models represented the passage of time and gave the presentation a thread of consistency.

The thirty-six looks that appeared between the bell costumes recalled designs from Browne's previous collections. The designer explained that he wanted to see how the suit has been 'conceptualized, pulled and prodded, in so many different ways over the past 20 years', so there was a profusion of canvassed coats and tailoring.[113] There were other familiar elements, notably knee-high socks, platform footwear, Hector bags and, for this collection, new Bermuda bags. Latex *trompe l'oeil* shirt-and-tie leotards, which spoke to the technical innovations of Browne's previous collections, were also worn.

Throughout, a nautical theme predominated. Talking after the show, Browne explained that the majority of the collection's looks were fantasies of the main character, played by Wek. She had entered the fictional train station 'thinking about her life and not being very happy'. The nautically inspired motifs – a lighthouse, jellyfish, starfish, scales, shells, seahorses, sailing boats, turtles, anchors – derived from the fact that the woman had been thinking of drowning her sorrows.[114] As with Browne's previous catwalk presentations, the audience would have been ignorant of these background details. Nonetheless, the show's melancholic undercurrent was conveyed through details that were clear to see, even if their meaning remained ambiguous. For example, the models' make-up. Eyeliner and blusher was applied in irregular swathes, with minimal blending and in bold contrasting colours of blue and yellow, which gave models an appearance of illness or anguish. Black lines drawn around their eyes and brows made some resemble Picasso's *saltimbanques* from the moody paintings that he created during his so-called 'Blue' period at the start of the twentieth century.[115] Hairstyles emphasised these forlorn looks. All models wore wigs that were attached to white bandages wrapped around their faces. The hair, in various shades of grey, was cut in styles that recalled different historical periods, notably the towering styles of the seventeenth and eighteenth centuries, and the bob cut from the twentieth century. The wigs were positioned at extreme angles as if they were about to fall from the models' heads. Perhaps an external sign of internal imbalance.

Two looks, apparently inserted at random, also spoke to the idea of malaise. These were the gargoyles. A common feature within the architecture of historic public buildings for carrying rainwater, gargoyles were conventionally depicted with monstrous faces and scaly, winged bodies. Browne's gargoyles were a lot less frightening, although their accompanying soundtrack, which sounded like something being scraped or dragged, was unnerving. The models' dresses were not identical, in design or colour – the first was dark grey, the second was white – but both were of two halves. The uppermost part of the garments was more obviously tailored, with a tunic collar and roped shoulders. The lower part of the dresses consisted of bundled swathes of fabric that trailed slightly behind them. Both models wore a gargoyle-shaped headpiece with pointed, twisting horns. Like the pigeon headpieces, these were also of two parts. Where one side appeared to be a complete gargoyle's face, the other side consisted only of a face outline, as though a final covering had yet to be applied. The complete face was on the left side of the first model's headpiece. It was on the right side of the second model's headpiece.

After the models had walked, each wearing two different looks, the porters who had earlier carried Wek's luggage returned. They moved up the runway from their sentry position, picked up the suitcases and, along with Wek, took up a position at its top, opposite the life-size pigeon-models. The traveller's train was about to arrive. The sound of a steam engine heralded the entry of a model, who wore a white train-shaped headpiece that resembled a mohawk. The show notes make it clear that this model did not represent the train.[116] Perhaps, because their ensemble was white and pale grey, they symbolised the steam and smoke of the locomotive? Their look appeared to be one of the show's simplest, and most ethereal, like steam. An unstructured three-quarter length coat with patch pockets was worn over a white thigh-length dress, much of its detail concealed. The model was followed by the train's conductor, who wore one of the collection's most dramatic garments. On their head they wore a tall, cylindrical white hat, decorated with a starfish. The headpiece was de-constructed, like all previous variants in the show, so only the left side appeared to be complete. The right side exposed the hat's internal structure. The model appeared to wear two mixed tweed trench coats that functioned like dresses. Their ensemble had a conspicuous A-line silhouette that effectively eradicated the shoulders. The garments were trimmed with a heavy gold braid. The outermost coat had epaulets that drooped because of the absence of shoulders. The coat was embellished with the nautical motifs that had appeared throughout the show. As the arbiter of railway time, each of the conductor's platform wedges was decorated with the same brass bell that had featured on the footwear of the bell-models.

After the conductor had left the runway, the show's final look appeared. The train. Walking up from among the *Palais'* fixed seating, model Grace Elizabeth wore Browne's interpretation of a wedding dress, a garment that had formed the finale of Parisian *couture* shows since the twentieth century. Elizabeth's dress was sheer white with a ten-foot trail carried by two white male models wearing white skirt-suits. The garment was based on a *Thom Browne* suit, but it was constructed entirely from layers of tulle and organza and appeared semi-translucent. The rectangular purse Elizabeth carried resembled a carriage. Four circular gold fastenings represented its wheels. The show notes explained that 'our protagonist [Wek] and train cross paths. [L]ooking back at each other if only for a second. [B]fore, fading into grey.' In a post-show interview, Browne explained that Wek's character had come to realise that her life was better than she had realised. Consequently, she decided not to board the train.[117] They had learned that a bird in the hand was worth two in the bush.

Conceptually, the plot of Browne's show was one of his more challenging. Journalist Ona Molas reflected that 'it wasn't until the end that you could understand the entire story'.[118] Browne has long claimed that he wants to challenge his audience's understanding and assumptions. A show like this raises questions about how much an audience can take in, particularly because they occupy a fixed, seated position with a limited and distanced vantage point. Much is increasingly made of the celebrities that occupy the front row in Browne's shows, and many turned out for this collection – including, Emma Chamberlain, Amber Kuo, Saint Jhn, Baz Luhrman – but when the likes of Dianne Keaton or Cardi B sit front row in their *Thom Browne* ensembles – Cardi B clutching a clock-bag from Browne's womenswear collection for Fall 2023 based on *Le Petit Prince* – it is unclear how much even these enthusiastic Browneans can really feel like they're part of what the designer does, particularly during a show when the narrative of the presentation is so equivocal.

Superficially, this show had a structure that has become recognisable, perhaps even characteristic, because Browne has employed it on previous occasions. Like many of Browne's recent catwalk presentations, this performance was divided into three parts, much like a screenplay. First, a set piece establishes the tone of the performance and introduces some, if not all, of the show's main protagonists. Upon their arrival, the characters typically interact with the set and highlight or introduce features that subsequent models will interact with. In the case of the *couture* show, the luggage placed in the middle of the stage served this function. Many of the characters within this initial segment remain on the runway for the duration of the presentation. Second, the development, or exposition, of the show, through which Browne conveys his main ideas. Typically, there is a repeating device, a specific sound or action often linked to time, that provides an internal structure to the section and helps with the organisation of multiple ideas. These ideas are typically conveyed using motifs inspired by America's preppie East Coast iconography. Third, a concluding set piece provides resolution, or at least a final statement on how Browne wishes his story to be interpreted. Within the first or final set-piece, or perhaps beforehand by way of props placed on the guest's seating, there is often an allusion to Catholicism. In the case of the *couture* show, reference was made before the show started, through the proverb from *Ecclesiastes*.

The development of a narrative structure is important in the evolution of Browne's storytelling because it facilitates more intricate and nuanced messaging, albeit messaging that is often challenging for live audiences to understand. For example, during the *couture* collection, there was a conspicuous colour change in the garments worn by the show's more symbolic characters. At the start of the show, the pigeon and gargoyle models wore dark grey. Towards the end of the show, both models switched to wear white and pale grey. This lightening of colour, which was emphasised by the dress of the model who may have represented steam, the conductor and the train, shifted the emotional valence of the show, and created a lighter mood. This reflected how the main character, played by Wek, came to find happiness in their life.

Above all, Browne's ability 'to weave this narrative and story in [people's] head[s]' seems to be predicated on an idea that has been emergent in many of his previous collections.[119] Namely, that happiness and an inner well-being are achieved, or most fully realised, through rigour and routine. Within the *couture* show, the regular presence of the bell-models indicated, on a superficial level, the passage of time as Wek waited for her train. Simultaneously, the repetition served an important narrative function. It provided a foil, an emphasis, for the undulating emotional experiences of Wek's character. The juxtaposition of looks that appeared bright and joyful, when they were embellished with starfish or sailing boats, and sombre and forlorn, when they were decorated with angular and geometric designs in darker colours, was clearer to understand because the bell-models provided the sartorial equivalent of a paragraph divider. Even with these twelve interpolations, *ShowStudio* editor Hetty Mahlich thought there were too many looks and too much repetition of the 'big sculptural coats', which began to 'lose [her] a bit'.[120]

Nonetheless, this presentation achieved a more convincing reconciliation between what have frequently seemed like contradictory and paradoxical aspects of his work. The story of Wek's emotional wrestling expressed more clearly an inherent Brownean idea that function and fun, darkness and light require each other to exist. Journalist Dhani Mau is surely right to observe that 'for all intents and purposes [Browne] already [did] couture' before this collection, but the greater emphasis on, and expectation of, material excellence seems to have enabled him to decisively articulate how the scrutiny and precision of his clothing's material forms facilitate and convey the internal and figurative joy that he enjoys and wishes Browneans to experience.[121] In previous collections, the maintenance of rigour, had often been conveyed through toned, statuesque models that seemed exclusionary. In this collection, perhaps because most of the models' bodies were covered, with their sex sometimes wholly unclear, there was a greater feeling of inclusion. A focus on one character's story of mental anguish enabled Browne to demonstrate that rigour, discipline and determination – concepts that have come to define his brand – are as much about people coping with the day-to-day as they are going to the gym and engaging in competitive sports.

The challenges of negotiating daily life were emphasised by the bipartite construction of the collection. This was evident with the models' headpieces. The split assemblage of these hats, with one side looking complete and the other looking unfinished, seemed to reference outward and internal states, or moods. A similar division was apparent in the de-construction techniques that Browne used for many of the *couture* looks. If upper parts were clearly informed by tailoring traditions, lower parts seemed unstructured, or were at least designed to appear so. These methods had been evidenced in Browne's earlier ready-to-wear collections, but the greater alignment of ideas and, perhaps, the creation of more looks, made it clearer that the materiality of Browne's world was not an end, but a means, or conduit, to a state of internal satisfaction and contentment. In this sense, his *couture* collection was at once one of his most fantastical and realistic.

Fashion commentator Bliss Foster has suggested the dualism within Browne's collection was borne of his desire to demonstrate that American *couture* could stand its own against French *couture*.[122] Browne was clear that he felt a 'responsibility' as CFDA chair to 'make sure people see American fashion in a very elevated way and at the highest level'.[123] The opportunity to define American *couture* in relation to Parisian *couture* also appears to have enabled him to clarify the key tenets of his brand. For example, Foster suggests Grace Elizabeth's 'wedding dress' enabled him to harmonise tailoring, which has come to define his work (through the shoulder-pads that were visible beneath the tulle), with *couture* (through the hip padding that were equally visible through the tulle). The coupling of these technical details demonstrated Browne's conceptual mastery. Foster also suggested that two looks featuring *trompe l'oeils* designs of women's breasts and a corset on their front were a conscious acknowledgement by Browne of the historic creations of French designer Elsa Schiaparelli, and thus another moment where he could emphasise his affinity with European *couture* traditions.[124] The style of the wigs, which seemed to reference French aristocrats of the *Ancien Régime* and American Flappers of the 1920s, may have been another occasion when Browne mashed together chronologies to indicate that styles from Old and New Worlds were conversant rather than contradictory.

If this seems absurd, a stretch, it seems important to reflect that this collection and its presentation was also one of Browne's most comic. Again, the apparent challenge of proving himself (and America) as an equal – or at least as a respected counterpart – to the traditions Parisian *couture*, appears to have encouraged him to clarify a defining characteristic of his brand. Its playfulness. From the moment the curtain lifted and Browne confronted his guests with 2002 cardboard cut-outs of an alternative Brownean audience, accompanied by the sound of rapturous, fake, applause, through to the appearance of pigeon-models and numerous *trompe l'oeils* designs, Browne used play and comedy in a way rarely seen with *haute couture*. *Couture* collections by Viktor and Rolf stand out as being playful, but their presentation is still largely conventional.[125] Through his show, Browne showed that his American sense of humour and sensibilities augment, even amplify, expectations of *couture*. His fun and fantasy provide a foil through which the discipline and detail of his garments is heightened.

Chapter 7

ARTFUL ACCESSORIES

Thom Browne and his world are beguiling subjects, in part this is because of the paradoxes that characterise them. The dynamic between fun and fastidiousness has formed the basis of discussion in previous chapters. In this final chapter, I shift the focus from collections and shows to objects. In doing so, I consider another defining paradox of the Thom Browne universe: character and commerce. The brand's collections are exquisitely crafted and defined by the designer's personality in a way that remains rare, even among luxury fashion brands. However, they have always been highly commercial. This is most evident in the *Thom Browne* collection of bags and footwear. The brand's bags, which have been described as 'eccentric arm candy', cross the divide between catwalk and sidewalk. In contrast, their footwear does not.[126] Most of Browne's collections are shown with elaborately wrought platform shoes, but the brand's commercial footwear offer to Browneans is conspicuous for its mild-mannered conservativism. By reflecting on Browne's bags, which traverse the threshold between romanticism and reality, and his shoe designs, which do not, it is possible to understand how such a characterful designer and his eponymous brand are able to reconcile character and commerce.

In his Autumn/Winter collection for 2016, Thom Browne introduced an item that has come to define his brand's range of accessories. This was a bag that resembled his dachshund, Hector (full name: Hector Browne-Bolton, according to a US *Vogue* feature on one of the fashion industry's most famous canines).[127] This initial design was truly imitative. The bag was fur covered and life-size. Since then, Hector has spawned numerous cross-body, over shoulder and hand-held offspring, one of which, from 2019, is now in the permanent collection of the Victoria & Albert Museum, London (Figure 7.1).[128] At the time of writing, *Thom Browne*'s online collection for men includes ninety-two bags. Two of these are in the shape of Hector. Of the ninety-seven bags available for women, seven are fashioned in Hector's image. If these do not seem large numbers, this reflects the quantity of bags, most in pebble grain leather, that the brand produces.

Online copy describes the Hector bag as a 'quintessential piece'. Thom Browne has suggested his bags are 'something important to round out [an] entire collection'.[129] He believes there is a need 'to have something in the collection that is whimsical [but made] really well – almost a collectors' piece in a way.'[130] And yet, for all the emphasis on craft and creativity,

Figure 7.1 Thom Browne 'Hector' bag, 2019. Copyright of Victoria and Albert Museum, London.

the production of bags is a significant moneymaker. Their price ranges from £1,350 to £4,440, depending on size and complexity of manufacture. Each bag was initially designed by a single Italian pattern cutter and they can take up to three days to complete.

In the year Browne introduced the Hector bag, *Women's Wear Daily* reported that his brand planned to double its accessories sales over the next two to three years.[131] As social and economic volatility has increased around the world during the new Millennium, global merchandising has remained a flexible, and consequently important, lever for *Thom Browne* and its parent company, the Ermenegildo Zegna Group, to pull. The designer's first *couture* collection in 2023 was notable for its commerciality, which was most evident from the inclusion of bags.[132] Whilst the Hector bag has been a starring attraction in this strategy, it was the first in a zoomorphic trend that has seen the brand produce thirty-three different animal bags.[133] Called 'Animal Icons', the range includes a deer, elephant, ostrich, rat and rhinoceros.[134] The spur for expanding this accessories menagerie was Browne's menswear and womenswear collection for Fall and Winter 2020 that took inspiration from the Biblical story of Noah's Ark (Chapter 4).[135]

The bags are not always practical. The snake, introduced in 2020 and updated in 2025 in blue pebble grain with gilt embroidered bands in place of the brand's signature 4-Bar design for Lunar New Year, seems particularly useless. According to Rodrigo Bazan, Chief Executive Officer of *Thom Browne*, the limited utility of some bags is intentional. 'Functionality is important but so is a very unique expression [...] I think the emotional part is important in the marketplace.'[136] Browne's outlook is similar: 'some are just beautiful design objects – that are functional in a way'.[137] In this conception, the function the bags serve is aligned to status consumption, rather than practicality.

The introduction of the Hector bag in 2016 coincided with rising interest among consumers in dress accessories that demarcated social status. Handheld bags are particularly adept at fulfilling this role because they are a form of 'handicap'.[138] By depriving their owner of the use of one of their hands, and conspicuously limiting their freedom of movement, the bag becomes a marker of how efficiency, one of the defining concepts of modernity, is being wilfully undermined. Consequently, the bag expresses the financial and social confidence of its owner. In this sense, the bag is mercurial. Its desirability is correlative to its impracticality.

The appeal of such an item to Browne, whose brand has oftentimes seemed an embodiment of the French maxim *il faut souffrir pour être belle* (it is necessary to suffer to be beautiful), seems clear. To carry a bag that is characterised by a diminishment of its main purpose – utility – demonstrates commitment to a sartorial vision and of living that transcends quotidian concerns. As ever with Browne, there is potential to read more into his designs than is warranted. He has also said asserted that 'the last thing I think people

need are basic bags'.[139] However, the mercurialism of his bags
is unlikely to be happenstance. Through Browne's reflection
that their creation is 'something I've been wanting to do, but
now I have the resources to do it; it's just timing – business is
really good', it is apparent that their creation is as much about
profitability as it is his personal expression as a designer. The
bags that Browne produces are a leitmotif for his world. They
embody the dynamic connection between rigour and play that
is integral to his brand's identity.

Browne's comment helps to explain why the footwear he
sells, and wears himself, has remained conservative. The *Thom
Browne* website currently sells sixty-four footwear variants
for women. For men, the different footwear options number
seventy-eight. These include boots, derbies, flats, high heels,
loafers, pumps, sandals, trainers, in shades of black, brown,
grey, navy and white. Absent are the platform shoes with brass
bells that appeared in Browne's first couture collection in
2023.[140] Absent, too, are the shoes with buttoned spatterguards
(or spats) that appeared in Browne's Fall and Winter collection
for 2020 (Figure 4.1). Like the brand's bags, these footwear
examples are 'beautiful design objects' and have no less a
claim to be collectors' pieces. Like the handheld bags, they
also handicap their wearer by constraining their speed, even
balance. Models waddling precariously have become a regular
sight on a *Thom Browne* runway.

Footwear that handicaps and proclaims the singular status
of its wearer has a historical pedigree. During the seventeenth

century, Louis XIV of France wore red heeled footwear to convey his divinely sanctioned status.[141] The monarch's *talons rogues* (red heels) became a symbol of the monarch's wealth and the inequalities that existed in pre-revolutionary France. Consequently, their wearing became increasingly untenable. This bit of history is important to explain why Browne's fancy footwear does not leave the romantic sphere of the catwalk.

Within and beyond France, growing acceptance of the concepts of efficiency, functionality and rationality, which were popularised during the Enlightenment and appeared to become facts of life as industrialisation got fully underway during the eighteenth century, meant that physically restrictive footwear, and the people who wore it – chiefly men at this point – were increasingly considered frivolous. The absence of any practicality, combined with their problematic political associations, meant that high heels or even elaborately decorated footwear, were an anathema. This attitude has died hard, particularly within menswear, and especially within the Ivy League and preppie looks, whose origins are privileged, conservative and, with a focus on athleticism, concerned with usefulness.[142] In their book, *The Ivy Look*, Graham Marsh and JP Gaul assert, 'The first thing a member of the Ivy fraternity will look at are your shoes; from there they check out the rest of your wardrobe.'[143] Sartorial conservativism continued to prevail in the United States during Browne's childhood and adolescence. In 1975, when he would have been ten, self-proclaimed 'wardrobe engineer' John T. Molloy published *Dress For Success*. Within his book, Molloy advised:

> Acceptable colors for business shoes are black, brown and cordovan. Patent leather is acceptable only for men in glamour industries, and I would question their use even there [...] In the most ultrasophisticated cities, shoes with tassels, or shoes with Mr. Gucci's rather chic initial are perhaps—just possibly—acceptable for some men. Elsewhere they should be studiously avoided [...] Multicolored shoes or those with high heels or platform soles should never be worn for business.[144]

Browne may not have taken direct influence from Molloy, but the inspiration he finds in preppie is nonetheless framed by a similar steadfastness around details, and the importance of function.

The footwear Browne includes in his runway shows is elaborate, even fantastical, and acts like a foil to highlight the rigour and craft of his brand's tailoring. Its function is bound up with the catwalk. Beyond this space, the footwear ceases to fulfil this role. Consequently, in the efficient, practical and disciplined world that Browne has created beyond the catwalk, his footwear has no place. For whilst his bags are, in his words, whimsical, their intended function is not wholly compromised, even in the case of the snake-shaped carrier (Figure 4.2).[145] The bags make a clearer statement about their owner's status than the footwear because through the retention of some of their usefulness they emphasise the choice that is being made to select beauty. They also emphasise how the construction of Browne's world is framed by a secure, if delicate, understanding of commerce.

CONCLUSION

During a twenty-year period, Thom Browne has grown his eponymous brand from a collection of five suits in Manhattan to a global business that produces up to eight new collections a year, including ready-to-wear and *haute couture*, for men, women and children. The visual appearance and personal discipline that characterises acolytes who wear the designer's clothes have led them to be called Browneans. It is rare for the followers of one designer to be designated by a catch-all term. The nickname is probably as celebratory as it is critical. However it is used, it demonstrates that Browne has created a world with a strong, clear connection between its underpinning values and material vision.

The values of Browne's world are deeply personal and can seem exclusionary. Browne's preferred form of communication is the monologue, rather than the dialogue. Through catwalk presentations, show notes and collaborations, he emphasises the importance that would-be customers should place in knowing what he thinks and feels. Oftentimes, he seems indifferent to how his views are received. The emphasis he places on physical proportion, both of bodies and tailoring, is exacting. The story of Browne upbraiding an employee who wore colourful socks might be apocryphal, but the designer has said enough in interviews and through show notes to demonstrate that his world runs by his rules.[146]

Browne is no tyrant. As the borders of his world have expanded over the past two decades, it is evident that his views, certainly their expression, have become more inclusive, both literally and figuratively. In his menswear and womenswear collection for Fall 2023, which reinterpreted the story of Antoine de Saint-Exupéry's *Le Petit Prince* (*The Little Prince*) (Chapter 5), he included Black curve model Precious Lee. This is a significant departure from early shows that featured a phalanx of white and toned models. In his first *haute couture* presentation (Chapter 6) he featured named models – Alek Wek and Grace Elizabeth – and threaded voices and experiences that differed to his own into his brand's storytelling. The theme of Browne's first *couture* show, which focused on a melancholic, perhaps even depressive, traveller, also indicated that he recognises that psychological strength is every bit as tough to maintain as mastery over the physical body.

It is as a storyteller, perhaps more so than as a designer, that Browne's role as Godhead has changed most notably over the past two decades. In his *Pitti Uomo Immagine* set piece of 2009, Browne demonstrated that he was a technically proficient narrator with a tale to impart (Chapter 1). But function and form were prioritised over fantasy and fun. As Browne has developed as a designer, and increased in confidence, his stories have become richer experiences, more nuanced and expressive. The development of a storytelling structure for his live catwalk shows, which consists of three distinct components, has facilitated this change.

Browne's storytelling, which connects him so closely to *auteurs* from the world of film, has been instrumental in clarifying the importance of America within his design outlook. This is not solely his homage to the preppie style, which became popular within menswear during the 1950s and 1960s, but his determination to have American fashion recognised as an art form that communicates and captivates on a par with European fashion. By embracing the Americanness of his brand, Browne's collections and their presentation have become at once more creative and rigorous.

The dynamic between form and fun has characterised Browne's work from the inception of his brand, but it is really only during his second decade that the paradoxical and deeply symbiotic relationship between these concepts has been articulated with clarity. The *Salone del Mobile*, 'time to sleep', presentation of 2024 (Chapter 1) makes this plain. A grey *Thom Browne* suit becomes a vehicle for self-expression because of the rigour and purity of their form (Figure 0.1). The ascetism of the tailoring can seem the perfect canvas on which to place joyful nautical preppie motifs, from whales to dinghies. In a similar way, the whimsy of a Hector clutch bag is defined through the disciplined skill of its construction and by the fact that it is worn with a sombre grey suit (Figure 7.4). This paradox appears to explain the internal logic of Browne's world, but it doesn't necessarily account for the growing appeal of this world over the past two decades. After all, however inclusive this domain has become, would-be Browneans still need to work hard and spend dearly to wear their red–white–blue stripes.

A possible solution to this conundrum is provided by the anthropologist Daniel Miller, who has tried to understand the appeal of another monochromatic garment, the Little Black Dress. Miller bemoans the 'gradual leaching out of colour and print' from women's clothing, such that 'the most [exciting] possibility left to me is to discover a new shade of grey.'[147] Unlike Browne, Miller does not respond to this situation with enthusiasm. To explain how 'grey and black have marched to the fore', Miller considers several factors, or culprits, but he ends up concluding that the popularity of the Little Black Dress – if popularity it really is – derives from the tyranny of choice. People simply become too anxious and weighed down by the options that exist for them when they go shopping that they opt for what is conventional, expected and socially approved. Miller concludes that psychological, and thus material, comfort is found in conforming rather than countermanding the fashion crowd. This is not so surprising a conclusion. In fact, it was pre-empted one hundred years earlier.

In 1903, German sociologist Georg Simmel argued that the growth of fashion and its industry was a cause for social concern because it stoked two competing, and ultimately unreconcilable, desires in people. First, an aspiration to use clothing to appear distinctive. Second, a compulsion to adhere to popular clothing styles to demonstrate belonging.[148] For all that has been written since, and however much the industry has expanded, Simmel's concerns remain at the heart of debates about the role and meaning of fashion in contemporary life. The concerns converge in *Thom Browne*. On the face of it, there could not be a more conformist, modest, quiet colour than grey and a more established garment to colour than the suit, which has existed in some form for over two hundred years, and is now as likely to feature in female wardrobes as male. And yet, for all this colour and this garment connote about conformity, through Browne's usage, they do appear unique. Through contrasting textures, subtle and dramatic changes of proportion and silhouette, grey tailoring enables its wearers to express their singularity. Consequently, it might appear that Thom Browne has been able to square Simmel's circle and enable distinction and conformity in dress to be reconciled. This would surely explain the growing appeal of his world. It also establishes why he is a fashion *auteur*.

APPENDIX

Thom Browne Timeline

1965   Thom Browne born (27 September) in Allentown, Pennsylvania.

1988   Graduates from University of Notre Dame, Indiana, with a degree in Accountancy.

1992   Moves to Los Angeles, dabbling in acting.

1997   Relocates to New York, working for Giorgio Armani and Ralph Lauren's Club Monaco.

2003   Launches eponymous brand, *Thom Browne*, in New York with a collection of five suits.

2005   Debuts first ready-to-wear menswear collection during New York Fashion Week.

2006   First *Thom Browne* flagship store opens in Tribeca, New York. Wins the CFDA Menswear Designer of the Year Award, and *GQ* Man of the Year. *Thom Browne* begins partnership with Brooks Brothers (until 2015).

2007   Limited collection for women.

2009   European debut for *Thom Browne* with a presentation at *Pitti Uomo Immagine*, Florence (see Chapter 1).

2011   Inaugural *Thom Browne* show during Paris Fashion week.

2012   Permanent womenswear line established. First Lady Michelle Obama wears *Thom Browne* for the second term inauguration of President Barack Obama.

2013   Wins the CFDA Menswear Designer of the Year Award for the second time. Recognised as one of the world's most influential people by *Time* magazine.

2016   Wins the CFDA Menswear Designer of the Year Award for the third time. Hector Bag introduced.

2017   First women's flagship store opens in New York.

2018   Ermenegildo Zegna acquires an 85 percent stake in *Thom Browne*, which is valued at $500 million. *Thom Browne* partners with FC Barcelona.

2020   First menswear and womenswear show held during Paris fashion week (see Chapter 4).

2021   Two *Thom Browne* ensembles from 2018 appear in The Costume Institute exhibition 'In America: A Lexicon of Fashion' at The Metropolitan Museum of Art, New York (see Figure 1).

2023   Begins tenure as CFDA Chairman. *Thom Browne* celebrates its twentieth anniversary. First couture collection shown in Paris (see Chapter 6). The University of Notre Dame teaches a one-credit module about Thom Browne's career, 'Strong Suits: The Art, Philosophy, and Business of Thom Browne'.

2024   *Thom Browne* stages its 'Time to Sleep' presentation at *Salone del Mobile* during Milan Fashion Week (see Introduction). Curates exhibition for Sotheby's 'Visions of America' auction (see Chapter 2).

ENDNOTES

1 Andrew Bolton, 'The Grey Manifesto', *Thom Browne*, ed. Andrew Bolton (London and New York: Phaidon, 2023), 12.

2 Kristian Olsen, 'Apply Now for "Strong Suits: The Art, Philosophy, and Business of Thom Browne"', *University of Notre Dame* (11 September 2022). https://ethics.nd.edu/news-and-events/news/apply-now-for-strong-suits-the-art-philosophy-and-business-of-thom-browne/. Accessed: December 2024.

3 Holly Peterson, 'How Thom Browne Launched a Multi-Million Dollar Fashion Brand from His Bedroom', *Wall Street Journal* (13 March 2025). https://www.wsj.com/style/fashion/thom-browne-interview-gray-suit-doechii-530ea42b?page=1. Accessed: March 2025.

4 Anon., 'Thom Browne's Entire Design Process, from Sketch to Dress', *Vogue* (26 March 2020). https://www.youtube.com/watch?v=VVbD2dXS4gw, 00.00.49 to 00.00.52 minutes. Accessed: September 2024.

5 Peterson, 'How Thom Browne Launched a Multi-Million Dollar Fashion Brand from His Bedroom'.

6 Raphaël Malkin, 'Inside the Mind: Thom Browne', *L'Etiquette*. https://letiquette.com/en/blogs/articles-magazine/thom-browne. Accessed: August 2024.

7   Will Welch, 'I Design My Collections While I'm Running', *System*, 22 (Spring/Summer 2024), 261.

8   Ibid., 262.

9   See, B. L. Wild, *Hang-Ups: Reflections on the Causes and Consequences of Fashion's 'Western'-Centrism* (London: Bloomsbury, 2024), 39–56.

10   Welch, 'I Design My Collections While I'm Running', 264.

11   Andrew Bolton, 'The Grey Manifesto', *Thom Browne*, ed. Andrew Bolton (London and New York: Phaidon, 2023), 12.

12   Christopher Breward, *The Suit: Form, Function and Style* (London: Reaktion Books, 2016), 142–148.

13   Wild, *Hang-Ups*, 121–122.

14   I am grateful to Michael Schreffler for his reflections on this point.

15   Anon., 'Tim's Take: Thom Browne', *Business of Fashion* (23 February 2021). https://www.youtube.com/watch?v=GK0q6H9cIOg, 00.25.50 to 00.25.52 minutes. Accessed: September 2024.

16   Ibid., 00.23.37 to 00.23.49 minutes.

17   Hannah Jackson, 'Welcome to Hector's World: Meet Thom Browne's Unlikely Muse', *Vogue* (14 August 2024). https://www.vogue.com/article/thom-browne-dogue-2024. Accessed: March 2025.

18   I owe this point, with thanks, to Michael Schreffler.

19   Scarlett Conlon, 'Thom Browne Shows How to Make the Perfect Bed with Theatrical Performance at Milan Design Week 2024', *Wallpaper* (17 April 2024). https://www.wallpaper.com/fashion-beauty/thom-browne-frette-homeware-milan-design-week-2024. Accessed: September 2024.

20 Anon., 'Thom Browne Fall 2009 Menswear [...] Pitti Uomo Immagine', *Thom Browne*. https://www.youtube.com/watch?v=BKPFUeGHlN4. Accessed: September 2024.

21 Andrew Bolton, 'The Grey Manifesto', *Thom Browne*, ed. Andrew Bolton (London and New York: Phaidon, 2023), 12.

22 Ibid.

23 Ibid., 13–14.

24 Ibid., 14.

25 *Pitti Uomo Immagine*, 00.12.53 minutes.

26 Anon. '[...] Salone del Mobile [...]', *Thom Browne*. https://www.thombrowne.com/uk/article/time-to-sleep. Accessed: September 2004.

27 Ibid.

28 Scarlett Conlon, 'The Best Fashion Moments at Milan Design Week 2024', *Wallpaper* (18 April 2024). https://www.wallpaper.com/fashion-beauty/best-fashion-crossovers-milan-design-week-salone-del-mobile-2024. Accessed: September 2024.

29 Jake Silbert, 'Thom Browne's First Time in Milan Was a World-Class Snooze (Exclusive)', *Highsnobiety* (18 April 2024). https://www.highsnobiety.com/p/thom-browne-salone-del-mobile-interview/. Accessed: September 2024.

30 Luisa Zargani, 'Thom Browne Stages Performance in Milan Unveiling Frette Collaboration', *WWD* (17 April 2024). https://wwd.com/fashion-news/shop-home/thom-browne-performance-milan-frette-collaboration-1236315937/. Accessed: September 2024.

31 Hannah Marriott, 'Far from Uniform', *Sotheby's* (8 December 2023). https://www.sothebys.com/en/articles/far-from-uniform. Accessed: November 2024.

32 Graham Marsh and J. P. Gaul, *The Ivy Look* (London: Frances Lincoln, 2010).

33 Jeffrey Banks and Doria de la Chapelle, *Preppy: Cultivating Ivy Style* (New York: Rizzoli, 2011).

34 Ibid., 115.

35 Marriott, 'Far from Uniform'.

36 Banks and de la Chapelle, *Preppy*, 142–143.

37 Chris Elvidge, 'In America: This Exclusive Collection from Thom Browne Is "What I Would Have Worn at Notre Dame"', *Mr Porter* (28 October 2022). https://www.mrporter.com/en-gb/journal/fashion/in-america-thom-browne-exclusive-capsule-collection-aw22-23566800. Accessed: November 2024.

38 Marriott, 'Far from Uniform'.

39 Andrew Bolton, 'A Common Thread', *In America: A Fashion Lexicon* (New Haven and London: Yale University Press, 2022), ix.

40 Ibid.

41 Andrew Bolton and Amanda Garfinkel, 'Discipline', *In America*, 136–137.

42 Robin Givhan, *The Battle of Versailles: The Night American Fashion Stumbled into the Spotlight and Made History* (New York: Flatiron Books, 2016).

43 Marriott, 'Far from Uniform'.

44 Joan Kennedy, 'Thom Browne to Curate Sotheby's 'Visions of America' Auction Series', *Business of Fashion* (4 December 2023). https://www.businessoffashion.com/news/luxury/thom-browne-to-curate-sothebys-visions-of-america-auction/. Accessed: November 2024.

45 Lucy Rees, 'Auction of the Week: Thom Browne Curates 'Visions of America' Sotheby's Sale', *Galerie* (12 January 2024). https://galeriemagazine.com/thom-browne-auction/. Accessed: November 2024.

46 Anon., 'CFDA: Defining American Style', *Sotheby's*. https://www.sothebys.com/en/buy/auction/2023/cfda-american-fashion-sale?lotFilter=AllLots. Accessed: November 2024.

47 Anon., 'Fashion Designer & Guest Curator Thom Browne | American Design with Sotheby's | Visions of America', *Sotheby's* (January 2024). https://www.sothebys.com/en/videos/guest-curator-thom-browne-talks-american-design-with-sothebys-visions-of-america. Accessed: November 2024. 00:00:47 to 00:0059 minutes.

48 See above, 15.

49 S. Bridges, 'Thom Browne's American Pie', *The New York Times* (6 September 2007). https://archive.nytimes.com/runway.blogs.nytimes.com/2007/09/06/thom-brownes-american-pie/:. Accessed: November 2024; Tim Blanks, 'Thome Browne Spring 2008 Menswear', *Vogue* (5 September 2007). https://www.vogue.com/fashion-shows/spring-2008-menswear/thom-browne. Accessed: December 2024.

50 Ibid.

51 Josh Patner, 'Thom Browne', *Time* (29 September 2008). https://content.time.com/time/specials/packages/article/0,28804,1844947_1845423_1845394,00.html. Accessed: November 2024.

52 Liam Hess, 'I Feel So Lucky That I Am Part of This Community,' *Vogue* (6 June 2022). https://www.vogue.com/article/thom-browne-on-growing-up-and-finding-authenticity.   Accessed: November 2024.

53 Georges Didi-Huberman, 'Before the Image, before Time: The Sovereignty of Anachronism', translated by Peter Mason, *Compelling Visuality: The Work of Art In and Out of History*, ed. Claire Farago and Robert Zwijnenberg (Minneapolis: University of Minnesota Press, 2003), 41.

54 Ibid., 32–33.

55 Ibid., 40.

56 Anon., 'CFDA and Vogue Join Forces for Fashion for Our Future', *CFDA* (8 August 2024). https://cfda.com/news/cfda-and-vogue-join-forces-for-fashion-for-our-future. Accessed: November 2024.

57 Ibid.

58 Anon., '*Vogue* Endorses Kamala Harris for President', *Vogue* (23 July 2024). https://www.vogue.com/article/vogue-endorsement-kamala-harris. Accessed: November 2024.

59 Rachel Tashjian and Maura Judkis, 'Anna Wintour Kicks Off Fashion Week with Jill Biden', *The Washington Post* (7 September 2024). https://www.washingtonpost.com/style/2024/09/07/new-york-fashion-week-wintour-jill-biden-nyfw/. Accessed: November 2024.

60 Anon., 'Thom Browne Spring 2014 Womenswear', *Thom Browne* (28 January 2016). https://www.youtube.com/watch?v=SI952kKREN0. Accessed: September 2024.

61 Kristina Rodulfo, 'NYFW: Meet Thom Browne's Elizabethan Clowns', *ELLE* (10 September 2013). https://www.elle.com/

fashion/news/a23714/thom-browne-spring-2014-womenswear-collection/. Accessed: September 2024.

62 Anon., 'Thom Browne Spring 2014 Menswear', *Vogue* (7 January 2013). https://www.vogue.com/video/watch/thom-browne-spring-2014-menswear. Accessed: September 2024.

63 Tim Blanks, 'Thom Browne Spring 2014 Ready-to-Wear', *Vogue* (8 September 2013). https://www.vogue.com/fashion-shows/spring-2014-ready-to-wear/thom-browne. Accessed: September 2024.

64 Tim Blanks, 'Thom Browne Spring 2014 Ready-to-Wear', *Vogue* (9 September 2013). https://www.vogue.com/video/watch/thom-browne-ready-to-wear-spring-2014. Accessed: September 2024.

65 Anon., 'Thom Browne RTW Spring 2014', *WWD* (10 September 2013). https://wwd.com/runway/spring-ready-to-wear-2014/new-york/thom-browne/review/. Accessed: September 2024.

66 Ibid.

67 Booth Moore, 'New York Fashion Week Spring 2014: Thom Browne Review', *Los Angeles Times* (9 September 2013). https://www.latimes.com/fashion/alltherage/la-ar-new-york-fashion-week-spring-2014-thom-browne-review-20130909-story.html. Accessed: September 2024.

68 Blanks, 'Thom Browne Spring 2014 Ready-to-Wear'.

69 Anon., 'Thom Browne's Entire Design Process, from Sketch to Dress', *Vogue* (26 March 2020). https://www.youtube.com/watch?v=VVbD2dXS4gw, 00.06.60 to 00.06.63 minutes. Accessed: September 2024.

70 Ibid., 00.04.36 to 00.04.43 minutes.

71 Alexander Fury, 'Thom Browne on the Story Behind His Creature-Filled A/W20 Collection', *AnOther* (4 November 2020).

https://www.anothermag.com/fashion-beauty/12930/thom-browne-fall-2020-fw20-aw20-collection-interview-katerina-jebb-artist. Accessed: November 2024.

72   Adam Geczy and Vicki Karaminas, *Critical Fashion Practice: From Westwood to Van Beirendonck* (London: Bloomsbury, 2017), 4.

73   Ibid., 2.

74   Ibid., 4.

75   Fury, 'Thom Browne on the Story Behind His Creature-Filled A/W20 Collection'.

76   Ibid.

77   Anon., 'Thom Browne's Entire Design Process', 00.06.30 to 00.06.34 minutes.

78   See above, 15.

79   Fury, 'Thom Browne'.

80   For further discussion of the 'Heavenly Bodies' exhibition, which informs this section, see Benjamin Linley Wild, *Hang-Ups: Reflections on the Causes and Consequences of Fashion's 'Western'-Centrism* (London: Bloomsbury, 2024), 114–118.

81   Samuel Hine, 'Playing Football with Thom Browne at the Home of the Fighting Irish', *GQ* (10 November 2022). https://www.gq.com/story/thom-browne-football-notre-dame. Accessed: November 2024.

82   Wild, *Hang-Ups*, 39–56.

83   'Fall Runway 2023', *Thom Browne* (no date). https://www.thombrowne.com/uk/collection/fall-2023-runway. Accessed: December 2024.

84   Mae Brennan, 'Strong Suits: The Art, Philosophy, and Business of Thom Browne', *Scholastic* (27 February 2023). https://scholastic.

nd.edu/issues/strong-suits-the-art-philosophy-and-business-of-thom-browne/. Accessed: December 2024. I would like to offer my grateful thanks to Michael Schreffler for reading a complete draft of this book, and for his considered comments.

85 'Fall Runway 2023'.

86 Vanessa Friedman, 'The Prince of New York: Thom Browne Offers a New Theory of American Fashion', *The New York Times* (15 February 2023). https://www.nytimes.com/2023/02/15/style/thom-browne-rodarte-altuzarra-new-york-fashion-week.html?auth=linked-googleltap. Accessed: December 2024.

87 Caroline Evans and Alessandra Vaccari, 'Time in Fashion: An Introductory Essay', *Time in Fashion: Industrial, Antilinear and Uchronic Temporalities*, ed. Caroline Evans and Alessandra Vaccari (London: Bloomsbury, 2020), 12.

88 B. L. Wild, 'We Need to Talk about Fancy Dress: Connections (and Complications) between the Catwalk and Fancy Dress Costume, *Fashion Theory* (2022), 26:1, 102.

89 Anon., '...Two Lost Travellers Meet...', *Thom Browne* (no date). https://www.thombrowne.com/dk/article/fall-2023-collection. Accessed: December 2024.

90 Ibid.

91 Ana Colón, 'Thom Browne Reimagines the Little Prince', *Fashionista* (14 February 2023). https://fashionista.com/2023/02/thom-browne-fall-2023-review. Accessed: December 2024.

92 Antoine de Saint-Exupéry, *The Little Prince and Letter to a Hostage*, translated by T. V. F. Cuffe (London: Penguin, 2021), 10.

93 See above, 31.

94 Saint-Exupéry, *The Little Prince*, 69.

95 'Fall Runway 2023', 15:19 to 15:31 minutes; Saint-Exupéry, *The Little Prince*, 72.

96 Jocelyn Noveck, 'Thom Browne Channels 'Little Prince' in Heartfelt NYFW Show', *The Independent* (15 February 2023). https:// www.independent.co.uk/news/ap-thom-browne-new-york-andrew- bolton-whoopi-goldberg-b2282485.html. Accessed: December 2024; Vienna Vernose, 'Every Look from Thom Browne Fall/Winter 2023', *CR Fashionbook* (15 February 2023). https://crfashionbook. com/every-look-from-thom-browne-fall-winter-2023/. Accessed: December 2024.

97 '...Two Lost Travellers Meet...'; Kristen Bateman, 'Thom Browne Sets the Tone for American Fashion', *W* (15 February 2023). https://www.wmagazine.com/fashion/thom-browne-fall-2023- nyfw-review. Accessed: December 2024.

98 Saint-Exupéry, *The Little Prince*, 82.

99 'Fall Runway 2023'.

100 Saint-Exupéry, *The Little Prince*, 85.

101 Friedman, 'The Prince of New York'.

102 Lauren Cochrane, 'Thom Browne Shoots Wearability to the Moon at Little Prince-inspired New York Show', *The Guardian* (15 February 2023). https://www.theguardian.com/fashion/2023/feb/15/thom- browne-shoots-wearability-to-the-moon-at-little-prince-inspired- new-york-show. Accessed: December 2024.

103 Noveck, 'Thom Browne Channels 'Little Prince' in Heartfelt NYFW Show'.

104 Cochrane, 'Thom Browne Shoots Wearability to the Moon'.

105 Bateman, 'Thom Browne Sets the Tone for American Fashion'.

106 Vernose, 'Every Look from Thom Browne Fall/Winter 2023'.

107 Bateman, 'Thom Browne Sets the Tone for American Fashion'.

108 Friedman, 'The Prince of New York'.

109 Ibid.

110 See Wild, *Hang-Ups*, 129.

111 Hetty Mahlich, 'Live Review: Thom Browne A/W 23 Haute Couture', *ShowStudio* (3 July 2023). https://www.showstudio.com/collections/autumn-winter-2023-haute-couture/thom-browne-aw-23-haute-couture/live-review. Accessed: February 2025.

112 Leah Dolan, 'Thom Browne on the Inspiration Behind His First Ever Couture Show', *CNN* (4 July 2023). https://edition.cnn.com/2023/07/04/style/thom-browne-on-the-inspiration-behind-his-first-ever-couture-show/index.html. Accessed: February 2025.

113 Ibid.

114 Ona Molas, 'Thom Browne Couture Fall 2023: A Bird in the Hand', *METAL* (n.d.). https://metalmagazine.eu/en/post/thom-browne-couture-fall-2023. Accessed: February 2025.

115 Theodore Reff, 'Harlequins, Saltimbanques, Clowns and Fools', *Artforum* (October 1971), 30–43; Benjamin L. Wild, *Carnival to Catwalk: Global Reflections on Fancy Dress Costume* (London: Bloomsbury, 2020), 85–97.

116 Anon., 'Women's and Men's Couture Collection', *Thom Browne* (n.d.). https://www.thombrowne.com/uk/article/womens-and-mens-couture-collection. Accessed: February 2025.

117 Molas, 'Thom Browne Couture Fall 2023'.

118 Ibid.

119 Mahlich, 'Live Review: Thom Browne A/W 23 Haute Couture'.

120 Ibid.

121 Dhani Mau, 'Thom Browne Hops on the Couture Train', *Fashionista* (3 July 2023). https://fashionista.com/2023/07/thom-browne-couture-fall-2023-collection-review. Accessed: February 2025.

122 Bliss Foster, 'The Kafkaesque Couture of Thom Browne', *Bliss Foster* (21 August 2023). https://www.youtube.com/watch?v=7XdoliJfU8w. Accessed: February 2025.

123 Dolan, 'Thom Browne on the Inspiration Behind His First Ever Couture Show'.

124 Foster, 'The Kafkaesque Couture of Thom Browne'.

125 Marissa G. Muller, 'Viktor and Rolf's Spring 2019 Couture Collection Is Full of Memes to Bookmark', *W Magazine* (23 January 2019). https://www.wmagazine.com/story/viktor-rolf-meme-couture. Accessed: February 2025.

126 Misty White Sidell, 'Thom Browne Plots Accessories Expansion', *WWD* (20 June 2016). https://wwd.com/feature/thom-browne-accessories-expansion-10459551/. Accessed: March 2025.

127 Hannah Jackson, 'Welcome to Hector's World: Meet Thom Browne's Unlikely Muse', *Vogue* (14 August 2024). https://www.vogue.com/article/thom-browne-dogue-2024. Accessed: March 2025.

128 Anon., 'Hector' Handbag', Victoria and Albert Museum Catalogue (no date). https://collections.vam.ac.uk/item/O1513286/hector-handbag-handbag-thom-browne/. Accessed: March 2025.

129 Sidell, 'Thom Browne Plots Accessories Expansion'.

130 Ibid.

131 Ibid.

132 Hetty Mahlich, 'Live Review: Thom Browne A/W 23 Haute Couture', *ShowStudio* (3 July 2023). See Chapter 6, 48.

133 Anon., 'Thom Browne's Entire Design Process, from Sketch to Dress', *Vogue* (26 March 2020). https://www.youtube.com/watch?v=VVbD2dXS4gw. 06:01 minutes. Accessed: March 2025.

134 Andrew Nguyen, 'Well, I Guess I Love Rats Now', *The Cut* (10 November 2020). https://www.thecut.com/2020/11/i-love-the-thom-browne-animal-icons-rat-handbag.html. Accessed: March 2025.

135 See chapter 4.

136 Sidell, 'Thom Browne Plots Accessories Expansion'.

137 Ibid.

138 Benjamin L. Wild, 'To Have and to Hold: Masculinity and the Clutch Bag', *Critical Studies in Men's Fashion*, 2:1 (2015), 43–54.

139 Sidell, 'Thom Browne Plots Accessories Expansion'.

140 See above, 48.

141 Philip Mansel, *Dressed to Rule: Royal and Court Ceremonial from Louis XIV to Elizabeth II* (New Haven and London: Yale University Press, 2005), 15.

142 Jeffrey Banks and Doria de la Chapelle, *Preppy: Cultivating Ivy Style* (New York: Rizzoli, 2011), 3–4.

143 Graham Marsh and J. P. Gaul, *The Ivy Look* (London: Frances Lincoln Limited, 2010), 22.

144 John T. Molloy, *Dress for Success* (New York: Warner Books, 1975), 159.

145 Sidell, 'Thom Browne Plots Accessories Expansion'.

146 Michael Schreffler informs me that Browne told this story during one engagement of the 'Strong Suits' course at the University of Notre Dame.

147 Daniel Miller, 'The Little Black Dress Is the Solution. But What's the Problem?' (2004). https://www.ucl.ac.uk/anthropology/people/academic-and-teaching-staff/daniel-miller/little-black-dress-solution-whats-problem.

148 Georg Simmel, 'Fashion', *Georg Simmel on Individuality and Social Forms,* ed. Donald N. Levine (Chicago and London: The University of Chicago Press, [1903] 1971), 294–323.

INDEX